**UPDATED EDITION**

# INSIDE THE BLUES

## 1942 TO 1982

### by Dave Rubin

Cover Photos:
Michael Ochs Archives
Tracy Hart (Stevie Ray Vaughan)

ISBN-13: 978-1-4234-1666-1
ISBN-10: 1-4234-1666-X

7777 W. BLUEMOUND RD. P.O. BOX 13819 MILWAUKEE, WI 53213

Visit Hal Leonard Online at
**www.halleonard.com**

# TABLE OF CONTENTS

# DEDICATION

This book is dedicated to my daughter Michelle, my wife Cheryl, and all those who love these blues as I do.

# ACKNOWLEDGMENTS

I would like to thank the following for their invaluable help in writing this book: Dick Shurman, Edward Komara, Nick Koukotas, Steady Rollin' Bob Margolin, Eric Leblanc, Zeke Schein, and, especially, the staff at Hal Leonard.

# ABOUT THE CD

The accompanying audio CD includes demonstration and play-along tracks for every example in the book. To play along with the full-band tracks, just pan your stereo all the way to the left.

**Recording Credits**:

Guitar: Doug Boduch

Bass: Tom McGirr

Keyboards: Warren Wiegratz

Drums: Scott Schroedl

Recorded, mixed, and mastered by Jim Reith at Beathouse Music in Milwaukee, WI.

# PREFACE

**I**nside the Blues is a four-part instructional survey of the greatest electric blues guitarists. I have presented their music from a practical standpoint in a way to make it accessible to rock and blues players. I have placed the emphasis on understanding blues harmony and its application to your music, along with the historical perspective that I am sure will broaden your appreciation of our only indigenous art form. Each volume is a complete entity, with the four together providing a comprehensive method for learning how to play the most important styles of electric blues guitar.

Electric blues is enjoying recognition unprecedented in its fifty-year history. With blues being the single biggest influence on American popular music, it should come as no surprise that it now has the largest and widest audience ever. From TV show themes and commercials to the flood of contemporary and reissue blues on the market, the music has finally found a conspicuous and permanent place of honor in our culture.

The blues has always been at the heart of the best rock. Though styles and trends go around in cycles, electric guitarists are looking toward the blues once again for the tremendous excitement and inspiration that comes from its enormous depth of expression.

—Dave Rubin
1995

# PREFACE TO UPDATED EDITION

**A** decade later and too many of the greatest electric blues guitarists featured in the first edition of *Inside the Blues* are now gone. However, as the immortal pianist Otis Spann proudly proclaimed, "The blues will never die." On the contrary, despite profound changes in the music industry, the intervening years have seen surviving legends like Buddy Guy and, to a lesser degree, Hubert Sumlin, reap the rewards of crossover acceptance. Young rising blues guitar stars like Albert Cummings, Tommy Castro, Deborah Coleman, Debbie Davies, Joe Bonamassa, Eddie Turner, Shane Henry, and Scott Holt may possibly warrant their own chapters in a future edition of this book.

The most significant change in the updated edition, however, is the inclusion of an audio CD. After countless requests from readers, I am happy to finally present this invaluable teaching aid. Play, learn, and enjoy.

—Dave Rubin
2006

# PART ONE: 1942–1952

*Gatemouth Brown, left, with Gibson ES-350 Premier and T-Bone Walker, right, basking in the glow*
*of his Gibson ES-300. Note that both men are smiling after a "Battle of the Blues Guitars."*

*(Photo: Michael Ochs Archives)*

The first decade of electric blues spanned World War II and the postwar years, a time of expanding technology, zoot suits, jive hipsters, and the transition from an agrarian to an industrial economy. Advances in electronics and vacuum tube design, accelerated by R&D (research and development) for the war effort, helped lead to the acceptance of the amplified guitar. The northern migration of African-Americans, particularly to Chicago from the South, provided a huge and appreciative audience for the electrified country blues that was a crucial link to their rural heritage.

Gibson, with their ES-150 archtop guitar and matching EH-150 amp, started the electric guitar revolution in 1936. Trombonist and guitarist Eddie Durham, from Count Basie's band, had attempted to amplify the instrument for years before Gibson's breakthrough and is credited with alerting master jazzman Charlie Christian to the ES-150 by 1937. Christian understood the potential of the electric guitar to compete as a solo instrument with the saxophone. In fact, he became so thoroughly identified with the ES-150 that people referred to the pickup on the guitar as the "Charlie Christian model." His recordings with Benny Goodman and the bebop jam sessions at Minton's in Harlem reveal the sustain and volume afforded him by his overdriven amp.

By the early forties, the pioneering and innovative Christian had been joined by Johnny and Oscar Moore, Tiny Grimes, Les Paul, Alan Reuss, George Barnes, Floyd Smith, and Al Casey on electric jazz guitar. When bluesman T-Bone Walker finally waxed eloquent on his amplified box in 1942, a jolt was felt nationwide. By decade's end, primal Chicago blues from Muddy Waters and Howlin' Wolf, the swinging Texas shuffle blues of Gatemouth Brown, the California R&B of Wynonie Harris, Johnny Otis, and Floyd Dixon, the Cajun funk of Professor Longhair in New Orleans, and the classy urban blues coming out of New York's Apollo Theatre by Big Joe Turner and Eddie "Cleanhead" Vinson attested to the new vitality.

All of the early electric guitars were either archtop or flattop acoustics fitted with pickups. Besides the prototypical ES-150, Gibson's ES-125, ES-300, the cutaway ES-350, ES-175, and ES-5, and the top class L-5CES and Super 400 appeared in the hands of those who could afford them. In addition, archtop Epiphones were also popular, as they were affordable and reliable. Muddy Waters recalled using one with a DeArmond pickup on his early Chess recordings. Budget-priced Harmonys, Kays and Stellas were often the pawnshop favorites of many itinerant bluesmen.

In 1947, another revolution got underway when Fender Musical Instruments of California began work on the first commercially successful solidbody guitar, the Telecaster. The added sustain and resistance to feedback that had plagued the hollow instruments helped push the electric guitar even further as a solo voice. Now, in conjunction with the relatively high-wattage Fender amplifiers, one or two guitarists working together could produce a sound big enough to take the place of an entire horn section, making small combos the perfect choice for the pervasive club scene. By the fifties, big band ballroom music was on the wane as bars, lounges, and roadhouses were bopping and rocking to the exuberance and power of electric blues.

*T-Bone Walker testing the inseam of his trousers while flaunting what appears to be a Gibson ES-5.*

*(Photo: Michael Ochs Archives)*

# T-BONE WALKER

T-Bone (Aaron Thibeault) Walker was born in Oak Cliff, Texas on May 28, 1910, and died in Los Angeles, California on March 16, 1975. In his lifetime, he saw blues develop from the quaint, parlor blues of the early twenties to the roaring rock of the fifties and sixties. In between, he witnessed first-hand raw country blues that fought its way out of Texas and the Delta, a highly emotional and driving music that would later become electrified in the hands of Muddy Waters. Most significantly, along with Charlie Christian and Eddie Durham, he was one of the first to acquire Gibson's new electric Spanish (ES) guitar shortly after it was introduced in 1936. With amplification, the guitar could now compete on an equal footing as a chordal instrument with the volume pumped out by pounding pianos and blaring horn sections. Even more importantly, T-Bone grasped the soloing potential of the electric guitar as he learned to spin out jazzy, lyrical single-note lines on a par with horn players. Musical history turned on its heels. Electric blues and, by extension, rock music owe their very existence to the power and finesse of Mr. T-Bone.

Music was everywhere in the world of T-Bone's youth. His mother sang blues at home and gospel in the church. His father was a sharecropper, but his mother remarried to a man who was fluent on several instruments and passed his knowledge on to his stepson, encouraging him to perform professionally. As a lad, T-Bone was one of the chosen few who had the honor of leading Blind Lemon Jefferson around the dry, dusty streets as he played for tips. Indeed, both the legendary Jefferson and the great Leadbelly were often guests in his mother's home.

By 1934, T-Bone was an experienced musician, married and out on the road with his own group. He was singing and playing and, when he could not be heard in those pre-amplification days, he would dance. Showmanship and entertainment would always be part and parcel of his gig, as he was a graceful and agile performer.

Eventually the rough life and violence of the juke joints, lumber camps, and barrelhouses became wearisome. T-Bone headed west in 1934 to urban Los Angeles and the unpaved streets of Watts. It was there that he came under the influence of the still-developing jazz and blues of southern California, what would later be referred to as "club blues." Pianist and silken vocalist Charles Brown was one of the pioneers of this upscale music, and the ambitious T-Bone joined right in. Still unamped, he became a singer and dancer with Jim Wynn's band.

By 1940, he was with Les Hite's big band, singing jazz and blues and starting to create sparks with his electric guitar in his off hours away from the bandstand. When Hite's touring band stopped in New York in June of that year, "T-Bone Blues," with Walker on vocals only, was recorded and released to minor acclaim. Apart from "Wichita Falls Blues," a Bessie Smith-like acoustic blues cut in 1929 under the sobriquet "Oak Cliff T-Bone," this was his official debut on record. Though he had been woodshedding on his new axe for several years, it was not until July 1942 that the electric T-Bone was finally recorded on "I Got a Break Baby" and "Mean Old World" with Freddie Slack's L.A. band. Both numbers reveal a remarkable degree of swinging sophistication. Walker appears to have left his country roots at home as swing jazz meets the blues scale in his playing. Echoes of Lonnie Johnson, Eddie Lang, and Scrapper Blackwell abound. Many of what would become T-Bone's trademark licks are on display, including his classic unison bend from the G to B strings that Chuck Berry would appropriate a decade later. Make no mistake, however, these in no way resemble amplified acoustic solos. Instead, they are fully-realized electric blues, reflecting the quick attack, sustain, and warm, reverberant, woody tone of the archtop hollowbody guitars available at the time.

The WWII and postwar years produced dozens of groundbreaking titles, with the epochal "Call It Stormy Monday" hitting the hot wax in 1947. T-Bone continued to record exciting, vital blues with bands large and small, name jazz and bluesmen, and pickup musicians clear through to the seventies. His classic period is generally considered to be between 1940 and 1954, however, when he cut over 140 sides for Capitol, Imperial, Black & White, and the smaller indies like Rhumboogie, Swing House, and Old Swingmaster.

Though slight in physical stature, T-Bone Walker was and continues to be a giant in American popular music. A man of immense talent and drive, fully cognizant of his worth, he was known to be generous and protective of his friends. He loved to gamble, and he lived the high life of cars, clothes, and alcohol. He thoroughly enjoyed the prestige of the Carnegie Hall shows and the tours of Europe. His influence on virtually every electric guitarist who followed him can hardly be overstated. Everyone from B.B. King to Chuck Berry to Stevie Ray Vaughan and beyond came under the spell of his "modern arpeggio" style while Jimi Hendrix (to name only the most obvious) was inspired by T-Bone's stage antics such as playing behind his head and dancing with his guitar. He was, is, and will continue to be the primary source for electric blues and rock guitar.

## SELECTED DISCOGRAPHY

- *The Inventor of the Electric Blues Guitar*—Blues Boy (Sw) BB 304
- *T-Bone Jumps Again*—Charly (E) CRB 1019
- *Plain Old Blues*—Charly (E) CRB 1037
- *The Natural Blues*—Charly (E) CRB 1057
- *Classics of Modern Blues*—Blue Note (US) BNLA 533-H2
  (Reissued on UA/Imperial (J) LAX-140-141)
- *The Complete Recordings of T-Bone Walker 1940–1954*—Mosaic (US) MD 6-130
- *Super Black Blues*—Bluestime (US) BXL 1-2835
- *Funky Town*—Bluesway (US) BL/S-6014
- *I Want a Little Girl*—Delmark (US) DS-633

## THE RHYTHM STYLE OF T-BONE WALKER

T-Bone's repertoire of chord voicings was not extensive by jazz standards, but it certainly lent an aura of smooth, urban sophistication to his blues. The following diagrams illustrate the main chords that he used to comp. The fact that they blend well with other guitars, keyboards, and horn sections, plus their moveability, makes them extremely versatile.

I Chords:

IV Chords:

V Chords:

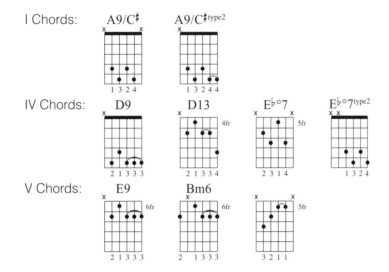

The A9/C♯ chord lacks the root while the type 2 version adds it on the high E string. Both are useful as primary I chord voicings. The E♭ diminished 7 chords are actually substitutes for the IV chord and resolve nicely back to the I. The augmented V makes a great intro chord, especially if it is arpeggiated. It resolves to the I chord as well. The Bm6 chord is a ii chord substituting for the V.

Track 1 shows a typical T-Bone slow blues progression. Arpeggiate the augmented intro chord, then strum the rest of the chords with a 12/8, or triplet, feel. Note the characteristic half-step moves in measures 3 and 4.

TRACK 1

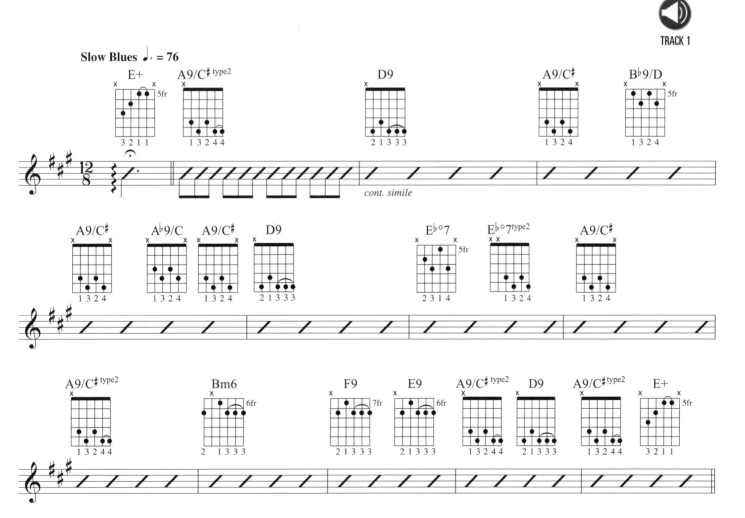

Track 2 is a 12-bar slow blues similar to "Stormy Monday." This type of progression, with its diatonic substitution of the ii, iii, and VI7 in place of the I chord in bars 7 and 8, had been employed by jazz musicians long before T-Bone. I have taken the liberty of adding in the kind of voicings (i.e., 7#9 chords) that a contemporary guitarist would most likely play today. Note that the B♭7 chord in bar 10 is a tritone substitution for the V7 chord that would normally occur there.

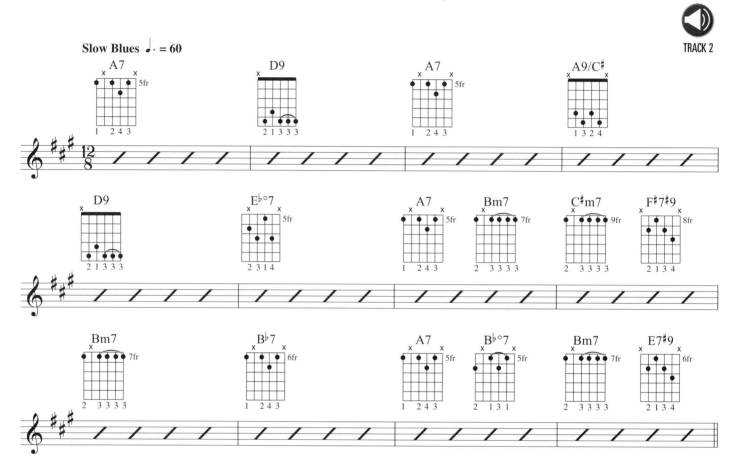

The A9/C# and D9 shown below are common chords in T-Bone's lexicon. They readily avail themselves to the kind of sliding embellishments demonstrated in Track 3 by isolating the notes on the D and B strings for the A chord and the notes on the G and high E strings for the D chord.

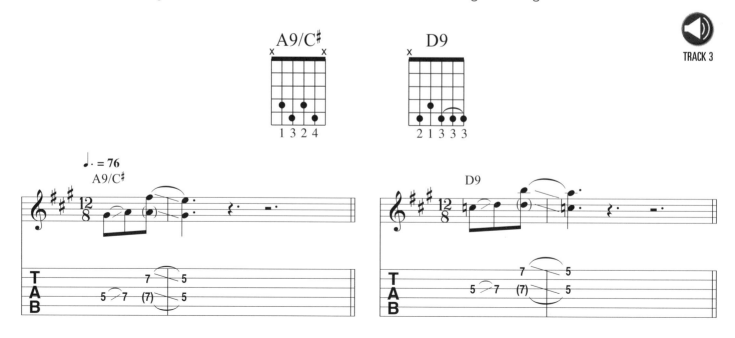

Track 4 shows a classic two-bar, slow blues intro that is indigenous to the T-Bone era. This type of unaccompanied intro is often played in rubato, or *free time*. I have indicated it in 12/8 time, however, for learning purposes.

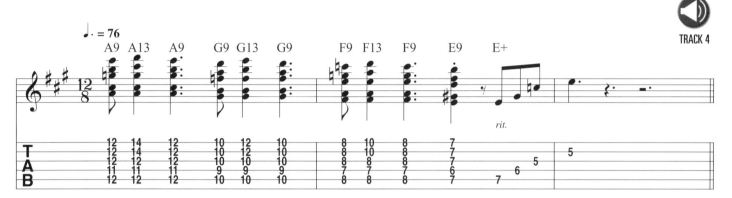

Jump blues and shuffles enjoyed great popularity in the 1940s, and T-Bone was a master purveyor of both. Though he often sat out of the rhythm section when singing, he was an excellent rhythm guitarist with an unerring sense of swing. Track 5 is a 12-bar swinging shuffle that contains T-Bone's favorite comping chord, the ninth with the third in the bass. I have arranged the progression with the moveable ninth chord supplying all the harmony. Note again the use of substitutions: the chromatic walk from A9 to C9 in bars 7 and 8, with the C9 functioning as a tritone substitution for the F# dominant (the VI chord); the B9 (II chord) substituting for the V chord (E) in bar 9; the B♭9 being a tritone substitute for the implied V chord in bar 10, and the descending chromatic pattern in bars 11 and 12 indicating a I–VI–II–V turnaround.

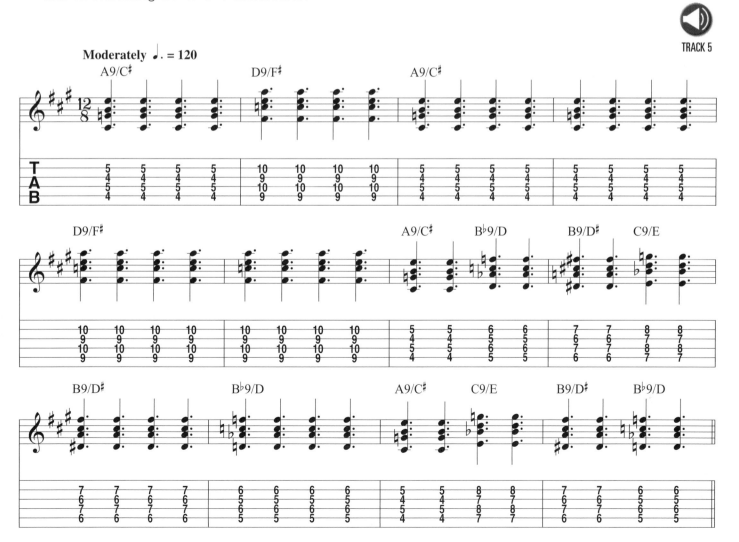

# THE LEAD STYLE OF T-BONE WALKER

While historians argue whether T-Bone, Charlie Christian, or Eddie Durham was truly the first electric guitarist, about one thing there can be no debate: T-Bone is the source of single-note, horn-type blues soloing. In addition, his phrasing was so expressive of the blues sensibility that it has come to define the style of every electric blues and rock guitarist who has followed in his dancing footsteps.

A diagram of the basic blues box from which T-Bone played almost exclusively for his entire career is shown below. This box, as well as its other four forms, are moveable to all keys. In the key of A, the notes are A, C, D, E$\flat$, E, and G (formula: R–$\flat$3–4–$\flat$5–5–$\flat$7).

A Blues

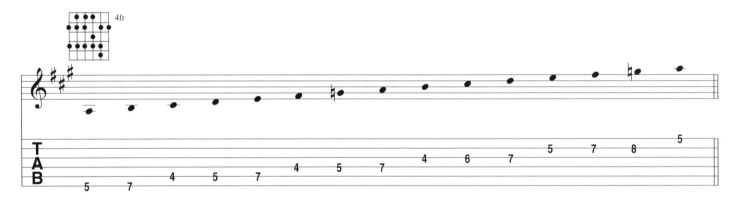

T-Bone would also alter the basic blues scale with notes from the Mixolydian mode. The notes in the A Mixolydian mode are A, B, C$\sharp$, D, E, F$\sharp$, and G (formula: R–2–3–4–5–6–$\flat$7).

A Mixolydian

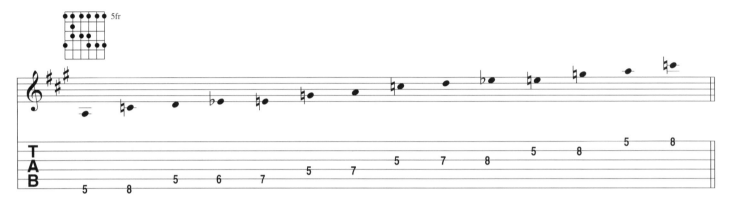

When you combine the two, a hybrid blues/Mixolydian mode scale results.

A Hybrid blues/Mixolydian

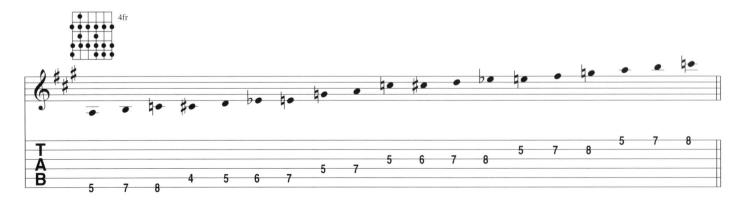

T-Bone's artistry was in his skillful manipulation of these notes into carefully structured blues phrases, not in mindlessly running up and down the scales. Rigorous investigation reveals fluid, swinging triplets throughout his solos and fills. Track 6 is a vocabulary of T-Bone-type blues licks, one bar in length, and broken down into which chord change they most likely would be played over. Be aware that many licks can be played over the other two changes, as well. Listening and analyzing the actual recordings listed in the discography will be your best guide.

## T-Bone's Favorite Phrases

*Gatemouth Brown windmilling on a Gibson L-5 with DeArmond pickup.*
*It is likely that this is the very guitar given to Gatemouth by the magnanimous Don Robey.*

*(Photo: Michael Ochs Archives)*

# CLARENCE "GATEMOUTH" BROWN

Gatemouth is a national treasure. Though known primarily as a guitar wizard, he was equally vituosic on fiddle and could perform with confidence on piano, harmonica, and drums. Along with a few others like B.B. King and Honeyboy Edwards, he was a living link to the pre-WWII days of country blues.

Born on April 18, 1924, in Vinton, Louisiana, Gate moved to Orange, Texas when he was a baby. As he grew, he absorbed the varied musical climate of a land that rang with blues, country, and western, cajun, and swing jazz. In a story that is as common to bluesmen as fleas are to a hound, he had the requisite musical mentor in his father who played fiddle, banjo, mandolin, and guitar. Gate began guitar at age five and fiddle at ten, even as he was coveting his brother's drums. In fact, his first gig was as a drummer, and at sixteen, he was out on the road with William M. Bimbo and His Brownskin Models.

After serving honorably in WWII, Gate returned to Texas, settling in San Antonio where he joined the 23-piece orchestra of Hort Hudge. When he heard how T-Bone Walker was wowing the crowds with his electric guitar, he picked one out and began to emulate T-Bone's swinging single-note lines. The first meeting between Gate and T-Bone has become part of the lore of the blues. Apparently Gate travelled to Houston where T-Bone was holding court at the Bronze Peacock, a club owned by the notorious Don Robey. Upon his arrival, Gate saw that T-Bone had left the stage due to illness, leaving his guitar lying there in his place. In a flash, he bounded up on stage, strapped on the guitar, and started to pick an impromptu boogie. The audience response was so boisterous that T-Bone arose from his sickbed in the dressing room to see what the clatter was about. Catching Gate with his axe, he leapt to the stage, reclaiming his instrument and his rightful place. The feisty T-Bone, never one to be shy about protecting his turf, threatened Gate and sent him packing. In later years, they would become friendly rivals, often engaging in many an epic "battle of the blues guitar."

The magnitude of Gate's impact in his club, plus his obvious ability, was not lost on the flamboyantly entrepreneurial Robey. In short order, he bought Gate a new Gibson archtop guitar, fancy clothes, and a plane ticket to Los Angeles so he could record for Aladdin Records. Though four titles were waxed, Robey grew impatient with the southern California label and bowed out of his contract with them after one year, preferring instead to start up his own label, which he named Peacock Records after his club.

Gate's Peacock recordings are the seminal work of his career and span the years 1949 to 1961. While the jumping shuffles and blues ballads owe an unmistakable debt to T-Bone, the Peacock sides have an energy and rawness that is startling to behold even today. Gate's phrasing is very much in the T-Bone mold, but his sound was more distorted and visceral, and he had a real aptitude for stomping boogie numbers. His backing bands tended to be full orchestras who could riff like the Kansas City bands of Count Basie, often engaging in call and response patterns with his guitar.

Never one to be pigeonholed as strictly a blues artist, Gate left Robey in 1961. In 1965, he headed east to Nashville to record a mixed bag of country, jazz, and blues. Since then, his recordings have consistently revealed his eclectic interests. He has played and recorded with people as diverse as *Hee Haw's* Roy Clark and rock singer Michelle Shocked. His recent output on Rounder and Alligator Records is as exciting and relevant to the modern musical era as his Peacock recordings were to post-WWII electric blues.

Long, lanky, and salty, Gatemouth Brown was a fiercely proud and independent man who had seen the up and down sides of the music business. He railed against descriptive terms like blues, jazz, and country, preferring instead to call what he does "American music." His live concerts were likely to contain one of his classic slow blues like "Dirty Work at the Crossroads," Ellington's "Take the A Train" and a ripping bluegrass fiddle tune. In addition, he would probably end his set with a blistering boogie shuffle, taken at a heart-stopping pace that would leave the younger musicians in his band gasping for air.

In 2005, he was diagnosed with terminal lung cancer. True to his nature, he refused treatment and intended to perform as long as physically possible. Unfortunately, Gate succumbed and died on September 10 the same year at the age of 81.

## THE GUITAR STYLE OF CLARENCE "GATEMOUTH" BROWN

As noted, Gatemouth had a penchant for boogie woogie. Track 7 is reminiscent of "Rock My Blues Away" and "Okie Dokie Stomp." The single-note melody line is based on the A Mixolydian mode and has the T-Bone ninth chord in bars 3, 4, 7, 8, 11, and 12. This piece should be phrased in a "call and response" fashion between the melody and the chords.

The F# note that ends bars 1, 2, 5, 6, 9, and 10 functions as the sixth of the I chord, the third of the IV chord, the ninth of the V chord, and the fifth of the II chord. Blues and jazz often use the sixth of the tonic as a common note to harmonize with the IV and the V chords, as well as the II and VI. Be sure to see that the C# (3rd of the I chord) is flatted to the C (♭7 of the IV chord, or leading tone) in bars 5 and 6. The flatting of the 3rd to the ♭3 to indicate the I–IV chord change is one of the most important musical moves in the history of the blues.

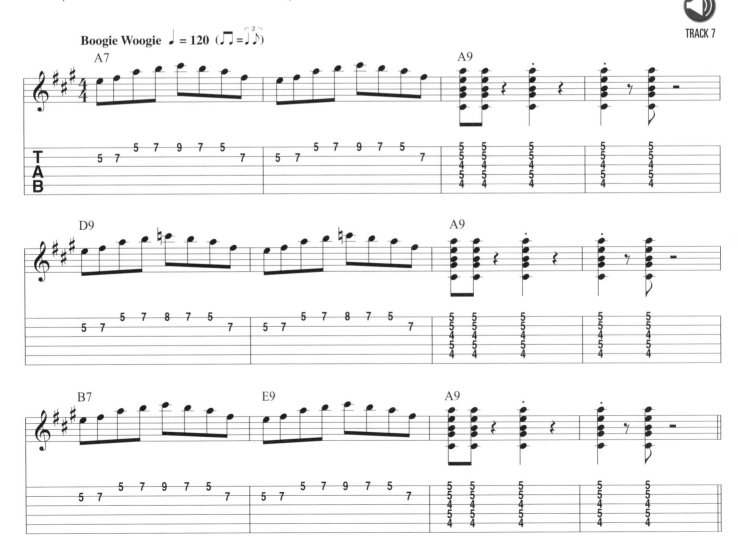

Track 8 is a variation on the kind of Mixolydian walking bass line that boogie woogie piano players like to play with their left hands. Gatemouth was fond of building songs on similar bass-string riffs. This is fairly simple and straightforward; however, the line in bars 9 and 10 that connects the II and V chords includes a very hip ♭5 (B♭) in bar 10 under the V chord. Do not miss it.

TRACK 8

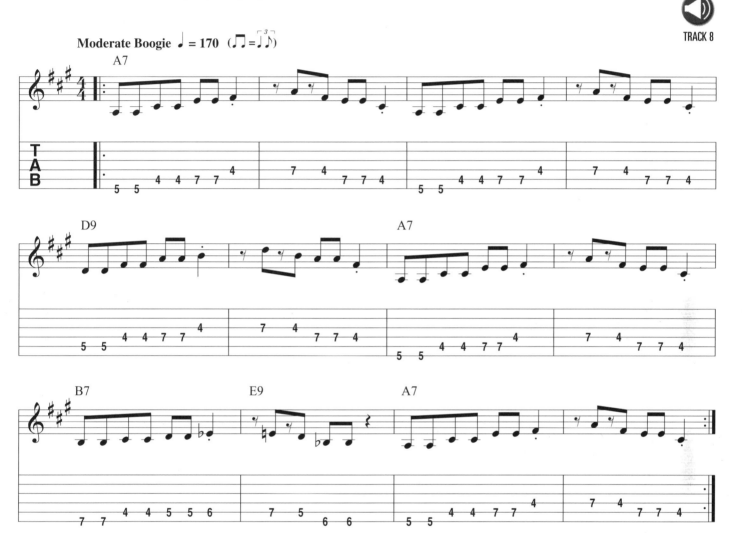

## SELECTED DISCOGRAPHY

- *San Antonio Ballbuster*—Red Lightning (E) RL 0010
- *Atomic Energy*—Blues Boy (Sw) 305
- *The Original Peacock Recordings*—Rounder 2039
- *Okie Dokie Stomp*—Black and Blue (Fr) 33.550
- *Alright Again*—Rounder 2028
- *One More Mile*—Rounder 2034
- *Real Life*—Rounder 2054
- *Pressure Cooker*—Alligator AL 4745
- *Standing My Ground*—Alligator AL 4779

**With Others:**

- *Rock N' Roll Gumbo*/Professor Longhair—Dancing Cat DC 3006

*Johnny Moore (left) and Oscar Moore (right) hugging their Gibson L-5 guitars (fitted with Charlie Christian pickups).*

*(Photo: Michael Ochs Archives)*

# JOHNNY MOORE

Johnny Moore's music conjures images of hip Los Angeles in the forties—palm trees, cool ocean breezes, double-breasted suits with fedoras, and smooth club blues as relaxing as a cocktail on a Friday night. Like almost all electric guitar players at the time and since, Moore came under the intoxicating influence of the mighty T-Bone Walker. Combining his jazz roots with swing blues and ballads resulted in a style more harmonically adventurous, if less driving, than T-Bone and Gatemouth Brown.

Moore was born on October 20, 1906, and died on January 6, 1969. By the late thirties and early forties, he had a trio, The Three Blazers, comprised of guitar, bass, and piano. It was patterned after Nat King Cole's group, the hot ticket in those days when big bands were starting to diminish after their heady times in the thirties. In 1944, Moore met singer/pianist Charles Brown, who had recently relocated to L.A. looking to further his musical career in the burgeoning southern California club scene. It was a fortuitous meeting for both men. After a period of rehearsals, they passed an audition at a local joint, winning out over twenty other trios. Johnny Moore's Three Blazers with Charles Brown would go on to write their own chapter in the history of postwar blues.

Though Moore had a recording and performing career after he and Brown split, the four years they had as a unit were by far the most productive and prolific for both. In 1945, they broke nationally with "Driftin' Blues" and in 1946 were named best R&B trio by *Cashbox* and *Billboard* magazines. In 1947, they cut the perennial Christmas classic "Merry Christmas, Baby." That same year, Johnny's brother, Oscar, who had been Nat Cole's guitarist, joined the group as a permanent member. Oscar had previously augmented The Three Blazers occasionally on record, and his swing jazz chops added another layer of musical sophistication.

The mutually rewarding pact between Johnny Moore and Charles Brown ended with a financial squabble in 1948. Though Moore retained the rights to The Three Blazers and would try a succession of new singers, the great Charles Brown could not be replaced. An era was ending, and by the mid-fifties, despite the efforts of stalwart Floyd Dixon among many talented others, the glow of Moore's spotlight had dimmed.

Even as an obscure figure in R&B annals, Johnny Moore has made a contribution beyond his famous association with the legendary Charles Brown. Jazz guitarists in particular, if they have any "bluesiness," certainly owe a debt to the silky chordal glisses, dominant runs, fluttering embellishments, and aural elegance that flowed so effortlessly from Moore's Gibson L5.

## THE GUITAR STYLE OF JOHNNY MOORE

Track 9 is an 8-bar, slow blues with a 4-bar intro in the style of Johnny Moore. The chord arrangement is as follows:

| Intro | | I | | IV | | ♯V | | V | ‖ |

| Verse | | I | | | | IV | | ♭VII | | |
| | | I | ♭VII | VI | | I | IV | I | V | ‖ |

It opens with a 4-bar run based on the hybrid blues/Mixolydian mode. The I–IV change in bars 1 and 2 is indicated by the double stop of a fourth (E to A), the dominant 7 note (G), and the resolution to the tonic (A) in bar 1. In bar 2, the 4th (D) and the ♭3 (C, the ♭7 in the key of D) contribute to the IV chord tonality. Measure 3 contains a triplet constructed from the C and D notes, which become the 5th and 6th of the F9 (♯V) chord.

The ♯V to V chord change found in bars 3 and 4 of the intro is common to jazz/blues. From there it is all dominant ninth and sixth chords in the verse. The ♭VII (G) chord in bar 4 of the verse is a substitute for what would be the second of two bars of the IV; in addition, it continues the cycle of fourths from the A to D to G. In bar 5, the ♭VII is used as a passing chord, connecting the A9 to the F♯9 (VI), which is itself a substitute for the I (A) chord. The half-step chord moves in bar 4 of the intro and bars 1, 6, 7, and 8 of the verse add an organic, bluesy feel to this jazzy progression.

TRACK 9

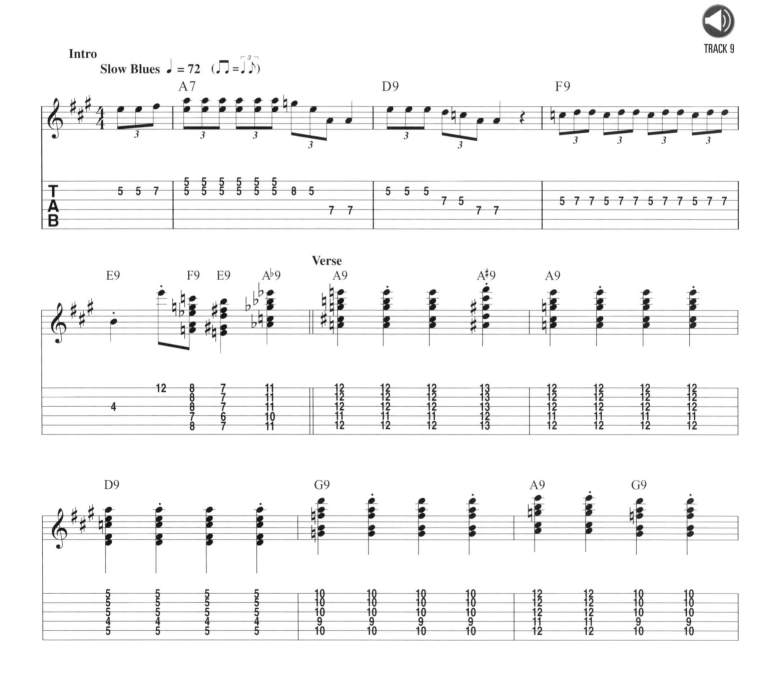

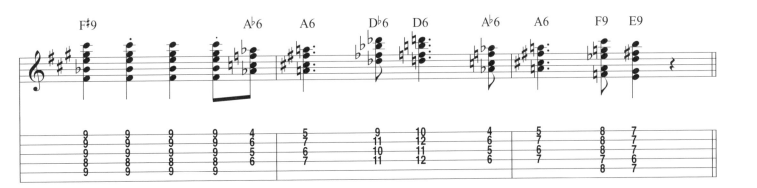

The slow 12-bar blues of Track 10 incorporates the kind of glissandi that are a hallmark of post T-Bone urban blues. Johnny Moore was a master at making these half-step shifts between chords an integral part of his comping. When listening to the original recordings, notice how the motion of the chords interacts dynamically with the fixed tempo triplets and scale runs of the piano.

The move from the E6 to E9 in measures 1 and 3 illustrates two ways to execute this form. As with most of the examples used throughout this book, these chords are completely moveable.

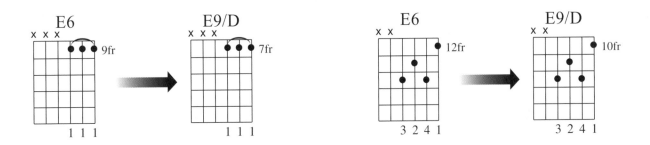

The three-note voicing is a particularly useful chordal fragment because of the ease with which it can be slid back and forth with the index finger. Be aware that context is everything in music. The E6 becomes an E9/D because the notes (low to high) D, F#, and B constitute an E9 inversion in the context of the E chord change. In the key of D, of course, the E9/D would be a D6. Alternatively, the E6 would be a C#m triad and the E9/D would be a Bm triad if they were played against those corresponding chord changes.

Track 10 includes a ii–V–I pattern in bars 9, 10, and 11. In this case, the ii chord is minor, as per the harmonized scale: I, ii, iii, IV, V7, vi, vii°, I. Diatonic theory, as observed in classical music, dictates the strict placement of major, minor, seventh, and diminished chords in progressions. As you have seen in some of the previous examples and will continue to see in the future, blues and jazz theory often ignores the rules of the harmonized scale. Instead, dominant chords are substituted freely for the ii, iii and vi minors, as well as the I and IV majors.

## SELECTED DISCOGRAPHY

- *Johnny Moore's Three Blazers*—Jukebox Li1 JB-1105
- *Why Johnny Why?*—Route 66 Kix-33

**With Charles Brown:**

- *Sunny Road*—Route 66 Kix-5
- *Race Track Blues*—Route 66 Kix 17
- *Sail On*—Jukebox Li1 1106

# CARL HOGAN & BILL JENNINGS

Carl Hogan and Bill Jennings are two of the more obscure electric guitarists in the history of R&B music. They were members of Louis Jordan's Tympani Five, the phenomenally popular jump blues and novelty band from the forties and fifties. Each was a gifted player, conversant in jazz and blues, and both men added their share of riffs to the early electric guitar vocabulary.

Carl D. Hogan, who was born October 15, 1917 in Georgia, joined Jordan's band in 1945. The Tympani Five (in reality, six or seven musicians) had been scoring R&B and crossover hits during the war years with the charismatic Jordan on alto and vocals, plus trumpet, tenor sax, piano, bass, and drums as instrumentation. When Jordan caught Hogan's act on the relatively new electric guitar, he quickly recognized the potential of another solo voice for his combo. Titles like "Beware," "Run Joe," "Inflation Blues," "Jack You're Dead," "Reet Petite and Gone," "Open the Door, Richard," and the all-time classic "Let the Good Times Roll," feature Hogan's melodic blues fills, solos, and deft comping. In addition, he appeared in several films with Jordan, including *Reet Petite and Gone*.

Little is remembered about Hogan other than that he was a tinkerer with electric guitars, coming up with a prototypical switching system for pickup selection. In 1948, he left the Tympani Five, fearing a loss of steady income when the boss of the musicians' union, James C. Petrillo, instituted a recording ban due to labor difficulties. He died July 8th, 1977 in St. Louis, Missouri. Though his tenure was short, he left a recorded legacy that would influence Chuck Berry and the beginning of rock 'n' roll.

James "Ham" Jackson, who recorded the cool guitar on "Saturday Night Fish Fry," replaced Hogan for less than a year, only to be followed by the powerful Bill Jennings, whose sliding double-stop solos and piquant fills embellished "Knock Me a Kiss" and the straight-ahead blues of "Blue Light Boogie" among many other titles. When Bert Payne took over his chair in 1952, Jennings went on to record with Hammond organ pioneer Wild Bill Davis. In 1954, Jennings signed with King Records in Cincinatti, where he waxed stomping R&B with baritone saxophonist Leo Parker and Jordan alumnus, organist Bill Doggett. Around 1960, he released two albums on the Prestige label with organist Brother Jack McDuff.

Like Hogan and Jackson before him, Jennings had a warm, woody jazz tone with the Tympani Five. His subsequent recordings from the fifties, however, exhibit a big, raw, overdriven tone that stands toe to toe with the honking saxophones with which he was often paired. Late in his career, the left-handed guitarist lost a finger on his fretting hand and switched to playing bass as a way of extending his vocation. He, too, has left a marvelous recorded repertoire for our musical nourishment, along with the Hogans, Jacksons, and other forgotten sidemen of America's classical music.

*Carl Hogan looking natty with his pinstriped suit and an Epiphone Emperor.*

*(Photo: Ralph Porter)*

*Southpaw Bill Jennings with a reversed, right-handed Gretsch.*

*(Photo: Frank Driggs)*

# THE GUITAR STYLES OF CARL HOGAN & BILL JENNINGS

Track 11 is patterned after "Beware" and is typical of the filigree that Hogan wove around Louis Jordan's vocals. Jump blues and early R&B, which grew out of Kansas City swing jazz, often used repeating riffs like this that could be played over the I, IV, and V chords. As with some of our other examples, this one is formed out of the hybrid blues/Mixolydian mode. The flat fifth interval, C/F♯, that is also heard in T-Bone's work, appears here as well. Though it most readily harmonizes with the IV chord (C is the ♭7 and F♯ the 3rd of D), it adds a bluesy dissonance over the I chord (C is the ♭3 and F♯ the 6th of A) and the V chord (C is the ♯5 and F♯ the 2nd or 9th of E). The double stop of a fourth (A/E) would later manifest itself in a big way in Chuck Berry's music.

The chords are the common dominant voicings found in the comping of Jordan's guitarists. They serve a particularly important fuction in this situation as they provide the cues to the changing harmony, inasmuch as the riff is the exact same notes for all three changes.

Track12 is similar to Jennings' solo on "Blue Light Boogie" and is harmonized in thirds. As in most jazz-rooted blues, the 3rd (C♯) is flatted to C over the IV chord to indicate the I–IV chord change. Whereas the previous example could stand on its own as a solo guitar piece because of the comping chords, this one needs the proper harmony underneath to bring out the V chord, for instance. The E/C is somewhat vague in implying the V (E), even in its position in bars 9 and 10 where you expect the V chord to appear in a 12-bar form. When an E-dominant chord is provided as support, the interval E/C assumes the 1/♯5 dissonance dear to the heart of blues.

## SELECTED DISCOGRAPHY

**Carl Hogan and Bill Jennings with Louis Jordan:**

- *Louis Jordan's Greatest Hits*—MCA 274
- *Louis Jordan and His Tympani Five 1947–52*—Jukebox LIL JB 605
  (Hogan appeared in Jordan's early videos and can be seen on a collection
  called *Five Guys Named Moe*—Vintage Jazz Classics Video VJC 2004.)

**Bill Jennings with others:**

- *Stompin' with Bill*—Gotham/Krazy Kat KK 838

The "Boogie Man," John Lee Hooker, with a Gibson ES-345.

(Photo: Michael Ochs Archives)

# JOHN LEE HOOKER

**P**ost-World War II America was starting to roll peacefully forward when John Lee Hooker's hard, electric blues hit the ground running. Forged in Detroit, his stark, steelyard sound pounded and clanged with the grinding intensity of Ford's assembly line, even as its context and modal forms drifted back to the Delta haze of depression-era Mississippi. The raw, over-amplified guitar tone that Chicago Blues pioneer Muddy Waters also used to slice through drum-driven, juke joint dances had become the primary instrumental voice. It possessed a physicality and sensuousness that was as primal as Abstract Expressionist Jackson Pollock's drip paintings of the late forties.

As the global horrors of war obliterated rural America's pastoral innocence, the economic incentives of steady employment in defense plants induced mass migrations from the South. The metallic noise of the northern factory towns was the clarion call for blue collar workers as well as musicians, artists, and writers. Out of this urban mind warp, away from the direct musical influences of Mississippi and Texas, came John Lee's butt-kicking boogie and brutal amp distortion. It would be one of the predecessors of the rhythm and rage of rock 'n' roll in the fifties and sixties.

The Hook was born on August 22, 1917, in Clarksdale, Mississippi. The fertile Delta was the spawning ground for many of the greatest bluesmen, including Charlie Patton, Robert Johnson, Muddy Waters, Big Joe Williams, and Son House. Hooker's stepfather, Will Moore, taught him to play and was his major influence along with Tommy McClennan. While in his teens, Hooker left for Memphis where he performed with slide guitar stylist Robert Nighthawk, in addition to singing gospel music. By 1943, he was living in the Motor City, pushing a broom on the day shift and pulling deep blues out of his amplified Stella at night.

1948 saw the official birth of the term "rhythm 'n' blues." RCA Victor retired the pejorative "race music" label in favor of the new classification for black music, as did *Billboard* magazine one year later. Waiting to help define this evolving style, like a junkyard dog straining at its leash, was Hooker with "Sally Mae" and "Boogie Chillun" on the Modern label. "Boogie Chillun," with its hard rockin' shuffle beat propelled by Hooker's stomping, racksaw guitar tone and rolling I chord riff, was as vital to the development of R&B as Muddy's 1948 recording of "I Can't Be Satisfied" was to Chicago Blues.

Forty years of recording on a dozen different labels under a gaggle of pseudonyms followed, with many of the initial sessions featuring Hooker flying solo. Second guitarists Andrew Dunham and Eddie Kirkland, in addition to harpist Eddie Burns, appeared on some cuts between 1948 and 1950. Beginning in 1951, with the requisite bow to commerical considerations, full rhythm accompaniment became the rule on record as well as live. It was not until 1959 that again he began performing as the lone troubadour of the blues. Chicago-style recordings followed until the early sixties when folkies "discovered" his music and welcomed his solo acoustic guitar (something he had always played on his own and on some initial waxings) or politely amplified electric. From the mid-sixties until the present, he has again recorded and performed almost exclusively with small ensembles.

Hooker is probably the most recorded bluesman, with his vinyl output weighing in at over one hundred albums. On these sides, he has enjoyed the presence of a veritable all-star team of sidemen. Ever the baseball fan, Hooker's first string would include his cousin Earl Hooker, Eddie Taylor, Jimmy Reed, T-Bone Walker(!), Willie Dixon, Otis Spann, Muddy Waters, Wayne Bennett, Phil Upchurch, Lowell Fulson, Robert Cray, Charlie Musselwhite, Bonnie Raitt, Canned Heat, and rockers Carlos Santana, Los Lobos, and Steve Miller.

John Lee Hooker's hip-shakin', neck-snappin' boogies and monochord, slow blues excursions are some of the most original and important contributions made to classic American music. His stone sober, talking vocals, which are the exact counterpoint to his guitar, and his "whiskey 'n' women" lyrics have influenced singers from Eric Burdon to Billy Gibbons. When rock musicians made their discovery of the blues in the sixties, Hooker's boogies became the jam of choice. Canned Heat built their live act around various "Refried Boogies." Norman Greenbaum's "Spirit in the Sky" and ZZ Top's "La Grange," to name two, owe their root–♭3rd–4th licks to the Boogie Man. Most significantly, Hooker's haunting, modal blues and tube-torturing distortion had a profound effect on Jimi Hendrix. "Voodoo Child," "Voodoo Chile (Slight Return)," and "Hear My Train A' Comin'" are the most obvious examples. "In From the Storm," though, besides being based on a repetitive blues figure, has the same type of call-and-response between the guitar and vocal as do Hooker tunes like "Crawling King Snake."

Hooker died on June 21, 2001 in Los Altos, California. Along with Muddy and Wolf, Hooker casts a giant shadow across the forties, fifties, sixties, seventies, eighties, nineties, and beyond. His free form and liquid meter are as mesmerizing and cathartic to the spirit as any classical art as they compress and expand the perception of time.

## THE GUITAR STYLE OF JOHN LEE HOOKER

John Lee Hooker and Muddy Waters have had the greatest influence on electric blues and rock. As opposed to most blues musicians who have one "style" that they nurture and develop over the course of a career, Hooker's music contains, amazingly enough, three separate branches that are equally important. The one that is foremost in the public conciousness is boogie woogie, and Hooker is the undisputed king of guitar boogie. It is an outgrowth of the piano boogie woogie promulgated by Albert Ammons, Meade Lux Lewis, and Pete Johnson in the thirties and forties. Whereas the piano masters built their songs from 12-bar I–IV–V chord structures, Hooker's boogies are usually nailed to the hypnotic repetition of the I chord, with occasional forays to the IV. Along with the epochal "Boogie Chillun," other titles from which the following examples are drawn include "21 Boogie," "Hastings Street Boogie," "Henry's Swing Club," "House Rent Boogie," "My Daddy Was a Jockey," "Momma Poppa Boogie," "Boogie Awhile," "Miss Pearl Boogie," "Boogie Woogie," "I Love to Boogie," "Shake Your Boogie," "Low Down Boogie," "Cotton Pickin' Boogie," "Do the Boogie," and "Boogie Rambler."

All seven boogie licks in Track 13 have pickup notes or phrases that reinforce the swinging, upbeat syncopation common to boogie music. As you can see from the notation, each one- or two-bar pattern is meant to be repeated. Also, in contrast to piano boogie, Hooker rarely uses more than the root, 3rd, 4th, and ♭7 from the Mixolydian mode, with the frequent insertion of the ♭3 into the bass line.

Hooker employs his fingers rather than a flatpick and uses open tunings extensively, particularly Open A and Open G capoed up to A. (Open tunings will be covered in the Muddy Waters and Elmore James sections.) I have chosen to notate all three of Hooker's examples in standard tuning as I find it to be most useful to modern guitarists, who may not wish to retune during performance or carry an extra guitar tuned open. Since he worked mostly in E and A in first position, it is easy to incorporate the open strings and droning E and A so prevalent in his music. (Please note: The *rhythm* is everything in boogie music, with the rests as important as the actual notes—and do not forget to tap your foot!)

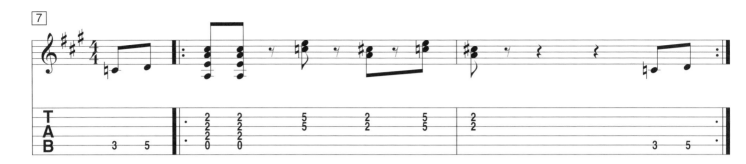

Track 14 is a fragment of a variation on "Crawlin' King Snake," one of John Lee's most famous "talking blues." This is the second branch of his music. In this kind of "stream of consciousness" blues, measures and chord changes are arbitrarily molded to fit Hooker's mood on the piece. "Wednesday Evening Blues," "My First Wife Left Me," "The Mighty Fire," "I'm In the Mood," "Build Myself a Cave," "Alberta," "Sailing Blues," "Graveyard Blues," "Three Long Years Today," and "Walkin' This Highway" are only a handful of tunes from this category.

Note how the chords in bars 2, 4, 5, 6, and 7 are placed in the middle of the measure rather than at the beginning or end, blurring the bar lines and contributing to the elastic nature of this type of vamp blues. The IV chord is present, but it does not appear as it would in a 12- or 8-bar structure. Fingers are encouraged to be used, instead of a flatpick, in order to approach the authentic rhythmic feel so necessary to the presentation of this music. Try the thumb for the bottom two strings (E and A) and the index and middle fingers for the upper four (D, G, B, and E).

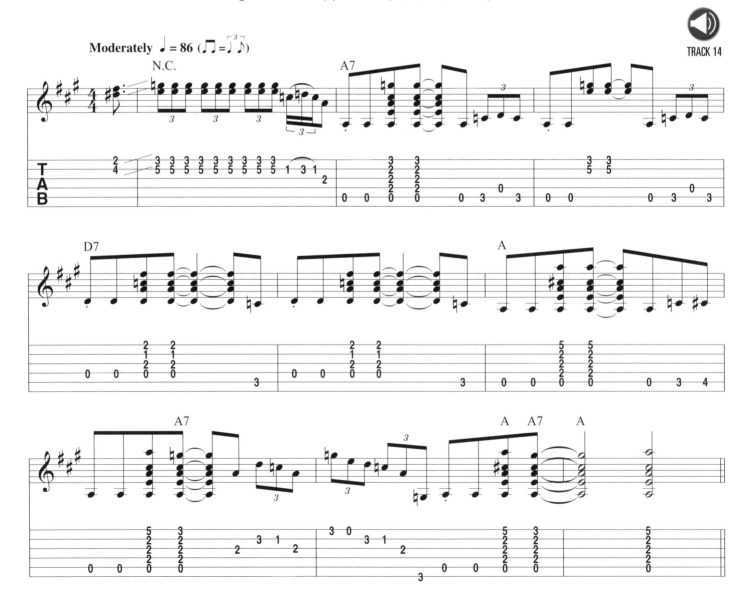

"Boom Boom," the Hook's hit from the early sixties, is the inspiration for Track 15. With few exceptions, 12-bar blues with full band accompaniment had become the norm at this point in his career. Other examples of this style of ensemble blues would be "Dimples," "This Is Hip," "It Serves Me Right to Suffer," "Whiskey and Women," "Big Legs Tight Skirts," "Back Biters and Syndicators," "Mr. Lucky," and "The Motor City Is Burning."

I have added double stops in fourths and thirds after each single-note phrase to imply the I, IV, and V changes. This progression could be predictable in its harmony, with the main lick ending on the root of either the I or the IV chord (E or A) in the first eight bars. Over the V chord (B) in bar 9, however, it ends on the A (♭7), adding a tasty touch.

These three examples barely touch on the length and breath of John Lee Hooker's recorded legacy. Extensive and intensive listening is recommended to fully appreciate the magnitude of his art.

TRACK 15

# SELECTED DISCOGRAPHY

- *John Lee Hooker... Alone*—Specialty SPS 2125

- *Goin' Down Highway 51*—Specialty SPS 2127

- *Gotham Golden Classics/John Lee Hooker*—Collectibles Col 5151

- *John Lee Hooker/Boogie Awhile*—Krazy Kat KK200

- *Boogie Chillen*—Official 6029

- *Is He the World's Greatest Blues Singer?*—Exodus EX 325

- *House of the Blues*—Chess/MCA CH 9258

- *Folk Blues*—Crown Records CST 295

- *The Hook: 20 Years of Hits and Hot Boogie*—Chameleon DI 74794

- *Boogie Chillun*—Fantasy 24706

- *Endless Boogie*—ABCD 720

- *Urban Blues*—Bluesway ABC BL/S 6012

*Muddy Waters bending the neck of his cherished Fender Telecaster.*

*(Photo: Michael Ochs Archives)*

# MUDDY WATERS

**M**uddy Waters was a son of a gun, a rolling stone, a hoochie coochie man. In 1943, he carried the raw emotion of the Delta blues to Chicago where he combined his mojo with electrical amplification to fire up the toughest, hardest blues for the next forty years.

Muddy was born McKinley Morganfield in Rolling Fork, Mississippi on April 4, 1915, and died in Chicago on April 30, 1983. He acquired his famous nickname from his sisters for playing in Deer Creek near his home when he was a youngster. When his mother died in 1918, he went to live with his grandmother near Clarksdale, the unofficial capital of the Delta. Mississippi has produced cotton, peas, and an extraordinary number of great bluesmen. The immediate vicinity around Clarksdale was especially fertile with Charley Patton, Son House, Robert Johnson, and John Lee Hooker being only the start of an illustrious roll call.

The first instrument to catch Muddy's fancy when he was thirteen was the harmonica, or blues harp. Before long he was gigging at local social functions and, by 1932, had taught himself enough guitar to work the jukes, suppers, and fish fries around home. After years of rambling and scuffling, Muddy settled on Stovall's plantation where folk archivist Alan Lomax recorded him for the Library of Congress in 1941 and 1942. Lomax had been scouting the Deep South for Robert Johnson's musical progeny. Everyone he talked to directed him to the young Muddy, who literally stepped off a tractor to sing and play guitar for Lomax. While he did indeed carry the legendary Johnson's bloodlines, he had never heard him in person, only on recordings. It turned out to be Son House, Johnson's teacher, who had instructed Muddy in the fundamentals of the Delta king's style. Country blues pioneer Charley Patton, as well as Blind Lemon Jefferson and Robert Nighthawk, were also influences. Muddy came away disappointed that the Lomax records were not for commercial release, but the seed to leave had been planted. Another hot, dusty year working the dark Delta soil would be his last.

The prewar South of Muddy's blues apprenticeship was a land of oppression, hound dogs, and hard work. The options of lifestyle were virtually nonexistent for a black man. You either busted your ass in the dirt or caught a freight train to the urban North where employment opportunities were plentiful and varied in the coming postwar economy. For a talented, intelligent, ambitious young musician like Muddy, it also meant the possibility of escape from manual labor altogether. Sounding out one of his sisters as to whether she thought people in Chicago would like to hear his music, she replied that she thought not. With an awareness of his self-worth and destiny that would come to characterize the rest of his life, he packed his grip and made his getaway.

The Chicago that confronted Muddy in 1943 was a cacophonous sprawl of stockyards, railroads, and mills. The confident country guitarist picked up an unloading job the very day he arrived. He soon found that the local blues musicians were hustling to cater to the entertainment and cultural needs of the Southside audience. Their's was a smoother, slicker city music, what Big Bill Broonzy called "happy blues." Broonzy, along with fellow plectrists Lonnie Johnson and Tampa Red, was in the vanguard at the time and gave Muddy his introduction into the blues community. He snared a gig playing acoustic guitar with Sonny Boy Williamson I, but found that the bigger, boisterous Chicago clubs overwhelmed his sound. Following the example of some of the other Windy City guitarists, he got a cheap electric box in 1944.

The epiphany of what electricity could do for country blues did not occur until after Muddy met Jimmy Rogers in 1945. They formed a duo with Rogers on harp and guitar, later adding guitarist Blue Smitty. As the need for a larger sound became apparent, more players were absorbed, with Rogers claiming future harp virtuoso Little Walter right off of Maxwell Street. Smitty split, but pianist Sunnyland Slim filled the vacancy with his 88s. When Baby Face Leroy Foster joined on drums, Rogers began playing bass on his detuned guitar, and the seminal electric blues ensemble began evolving.

In 1946, Muddy recorded three tracks for Columbia that remained in the can until 1971. Again in 1947, he waxed musical on four cuts, this time for Aristocrat Records. Two selections were Sunnyland's and two, "Gypsy Woman" and "Little Anna Mae," were cast under his name. These were squarely in the T-Bone Walker mode of swing blues, but Aristocrat co-owner Leonard Chess was unimpressed by Muddy's cool, single-string solos and fills. In 1948, however, a wary Chess was convinced into letting him try a couple of tunes the way he had been playing in the clubs. The result was "I Can't Be Satisfied" b/w "Feel Like Going Home." Both sides had been recorded acoustically for Lomax fifteen years earlier, but here they were presented in Muddy's whomping electric Delta slide guitar style with Big Crawford backing him on bass fiddle. To almost everyone's utter amazement, the record became a huge hit in the black community and the first commercial success for the Chess brothers. An audience of country people who had immigrated to the big city hungered for a taste of home, and Leonard and Muddy gave it to them straight and hot.

Meanwhile, Muddy continued to rework his Delta themes with his raucous electric blues group in the teeming, noisy Southside clubs. They rocked the house, gaining a reputation as "The Headhunters" as they bested other bands in cutting contests. Muddy desperately wanted to record his band, but the cautious Chess was adamant about not messing with what he perceived as the winning combination of electric guitar and stand-up, doghouse bass. In 1949, drummer Baby Face Foster quietly added second guitar on four more Aristocrat songs. In 1950, Johnny Jones's piano joined Foster's drums, Crawford's bass, and Muddy's big-toned electric slide on "Screamin' and Cryin'." The progress towards a full electric blues combo would not be denied.

The same year, Leonard Chess left Aristocrat Records and, with his brother Phil, formed Chess Records. "Rolling Stone" b/w "Walkin' Blues" was released and became the first hit for the new company. A historic partnership between Muddy and Chess was formed out of mutual respect and economic incentive. In 1951, Jimmy Rogers, sideman deluxe, was brought in on guitar, and the classic line-up of two guitars, bass, and drums, with various combinations of harp and piano, became reality. The blueprint for future blues and rock bands was finally drafted and off the drawing board.

Through 1953, the small country group (sans piano and, sometimes, bass) persisted with classics like "Long Distance Call" and "Still a Fool." September of that year saw "Blow Wind Blow" with Muddy (guitar and vocals), Jimmy Rogers (guitar), Otis Spann (piano), Walter "Shakey" Horton (harp), and Elgin Evans (drums). Spann and Evans added a new element of swinging, rhythmic drive to the deep, down-home feel of the original band. Then, in 1954, with the magic Little Walter Jacobs back, "Hoochie Coochie Man" was sprung on an unsuspecting music world, and another new direction in blues was heralded. Master blues composer Willie Dixon penned the opus and played bass, freeing Rogers to play stellar rhythm and fill guitar. The first, and perhaps best, version of the mature Muddy Waters band had arrived, and the music rocked with the energy of big city dynamism and country funk.

An accidental hand injury took the guitar away from Muddy in the late fifties and early sixties. The recordings continued with two guitars, as a first-class stable of replacements was established to fill the positions. Besides Jimmy Rogers, there was Pat Hare, Luther Tucker, and Andrew Stephens from which to choose. Earl Hooker and Buddy Guy also left their highly individual stamps on modern Chicago blues standards like "You Shook Me" and "The Same Thing." Around the mid-sixties, Muddy picked up his axe again. He was playing better than ever as the acoustic sides "Good Morning Little Schoolgirl," "My Home in the Delta," and the fierce electric slide of "You Can't Lose What You Never Had" firmly attest to on *Folk Singer* in 1963.

The late sixties saw Muddy riding the crest of the blues revival on stage, but his recorded output was checkered. *Electric Mud* and *After the Rain* were low water marks with their ridiculous wah-wahs and fuzztones. *Fathers and Sons,* though, with the young turks Michael Bloomfield, Paul Butterfield, and Donald "Duck" Dunn, was a sweetly satisfying, authentic survey of Muddy's choice material. Such a loving, empathetic approach to recording Muddy would not occur again until Johnny Winter's successful collaboration from 1977 through 1981 for Blue Sky Records. Plans were taking shape for still more recordings at the time of Muddy's death in 1983.

Though never a virtuoso soloist, Muddy had an intuitive sense of the power and expressive possibilities of amplifier distortion. The Aristocrat and early Chess sides would be diminished considerably without the thumping bass notes and fat, sustaining treble licks afforded by overdriven vacuum tubes. He clearly said it with his sound as well as his choice of notes. Muddy was a man of commanding vocal presence with a guitar voice big and bad enough to go toe-to-toe with any of the pickers who played with him.

Muddy did not listen to other guitarists outside of the men from his generation. He most certainly was not impressed by fast, flashy players, though he respected the likes of Johnny Winter and Bob Margolin. What he looked for in any blues musican was the ability to play "delay time," or behind the beat. When asked in later years if he ever felt the need to practice, he replied, "No. I've been playing the blues for fifty years; it's in my hands. I don't need to practice it." It was also in his head and heart, and there will never be another like him.

## SELECTED DISCOGRAPHY

- *The Chess Box*—CH6 80002
- *Muddy Waters Down on Stovall's Plantation*—Testament Records T 2210
- *Rare and Unissued*—Chess CH 9180
- *Trouble No More*—Chess CH 9291
- *Fathers and Sons*—Frog Records a BRP 22010 (Reissued on Chess)
- *Hard Again*—Blue Sky X698
- *Folk Singer*—Chess LP 1483

## COUNTRY BLUES

In Chicago in the late forties and early fifties, Muddy was playing amplified guitar in a style that was directly related to the acoustic Delta blues that he had performed in Mississippi a decade before. In contrast to some country blues guitarists who could only play in open tunings, Muddy was capable of playing with authority in standard tuning as well. Track 16 is rendered in the manner of songs like "Rolling Stone" and "Still a Fool," the latter of which is capoed up a fret to the key of F in the original version.

This piece could be played with a flatpick or fingerstyle. It is important to emphasize the downbeats in each measure as they give the sense of rhythmic accompaniment that is so essential to solo blues. In most measures, these notes are the roots of each chord change.

Another characteristic of country or Delta blues is the dynamic contrast between measures where full chords are used, and where a sparse outline of notes indicate the change. The open position A7 chord in bars 5 and 6 anchors the middle of the chord progression, while mainly single-note runs imply the rest of the harmony throughout. The inferred B7 in bar 9 is pared to the bare minimum as it contains the root (B) and the fifth (F$\sharp$). Bar 10 follows with a bass-string run in A that connects the root (A) with the fifth (E), returning back to the root before resolving to the tonic for the start of the turnaround.

The double-stop pull-offs over the E chord in bars 1–4 should be played by using the index finger as a partial barre.

# SLIDE GUITAR—STANDARD TUNING

Like the immortal Robert Nighthawk, Muddy played slide in both standard and open tuning.

Because the chordal harmony is limited in standard-tuned slide, it is imperative to know where the major triads are located. Below are the E (I), A (IV), and B (V) triads as they would be played over the fret wire.

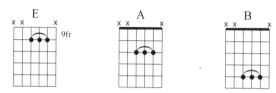

NOTE: A and B could also be accessed at frets 14 and 16, respectively.

When combined with the related chord tones shown below, the triads give a strong tonal center around which the appropriate harmony can be built for each chord change. The notes indicated are, low to high, root, 3rd, 5th, and octave. (Be sure to see that the two low notes in each box below overlap with the two notes on the G and B strings from each respective triad above.)

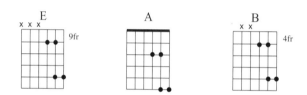

While notes from the other positions of the blues scale can be played, these forms are perhaps the most useful as a basis to work around.

The 12-bar progression with intro in Track 17 is similar to "Walkin' Blues," "Honey Bee," "Long Distance Call," and "I Feel Like Going Home." It is a combination of fretted notes and slide in standard tuning. I suggest wearing the slide on the pinky so as to free up the other fingers to fret individual notes and chords.

The intro is classic Muddy Waters with the slurry bend in bar 1, the slippery triplet figure in bar 4 (based around the E triad), and the measure of 2/4 (!) time in bar 3 for a total of five bars. In real time, though, it actually feels like 4½ bars. The Delta tradition that Muddy grew out of frequently mixed time signatures and was not constrained by even numbers when it came to verses and intros. Many country blues have 11-, 12½- or 13-bar verses, for example. As these people often performed alone, they could expand or compress chord structures to suit their lyric or musical content.

Like the previous example, this progression contains only two bars of chords, with single-note phrases and dyads predominating. The triple-stop E7 in measure 6 that moves by half step to become an implied A7 in bar 7 is a staple of Muddy's style. Theoretically, half-step movement could indicate an E°7 chord (G=♭3, B♭=♭5, D♭=♭♭7)—minus the E root. However, in a blues context, the notes function as G=♭7, B♭=♭9 and C♯=3 in the key of A, implying an A dominant chord. This harmonic device goes back at least as far as Robert Johnson, was employed regularly by Muddy, and has become an accepted part of the blues vocabulary to indicate a I–IV change.

Some of the harmony expressed here is more sophisticated than in Track 16. In particular, the root and flat 7 (as opposed to the more pedestrian root and fifth) is used in bars 10 (A7) and 14 (B7), thereby imparting a more dominant flavor.

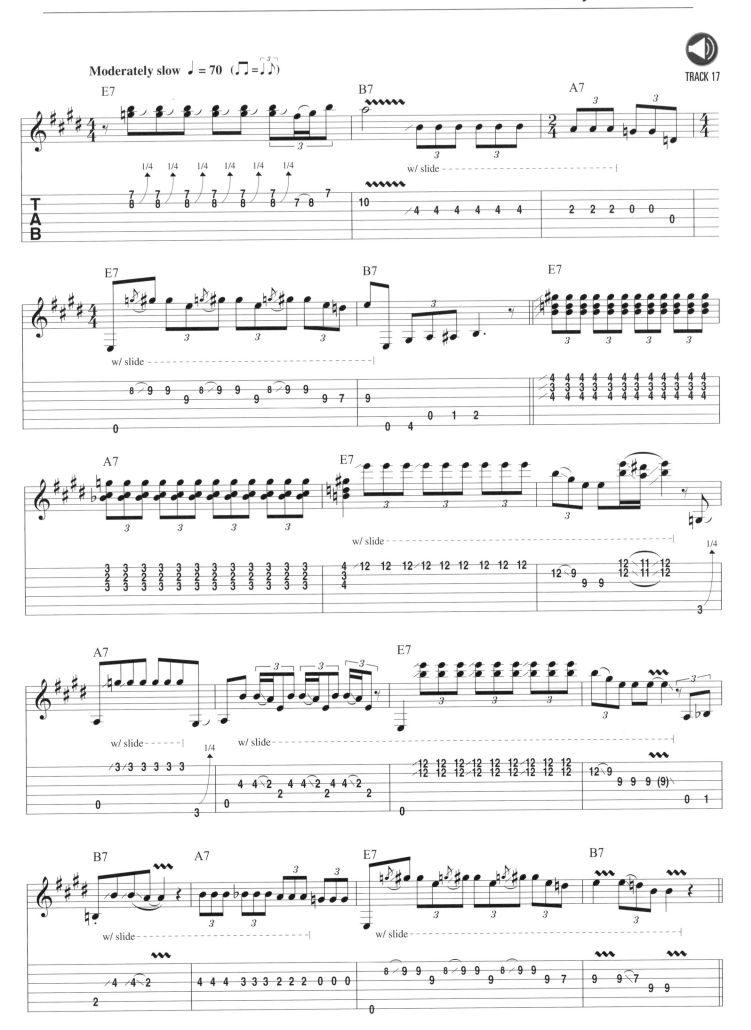

TRACK 17

# SLIDE GUITAR—OPEN TUNING

The two most common open tunings in blues are G and D. Open G tends to sound softer, more country-like than Open D, which conveys the hard urban sound found in the music of Elmore James. This is because Open G emphasizes the more melodic chordal intervals of a third (G–B, B–D) on the top strings. In contrast, Open D emphasizes fourths (A–D), which sound pentatonic or bluesy in nature. Muddy played mainly in G, with a capo often applied to change keys.

Below are the open strings in standard tuning (low to high) alongside the open strings in Open G. I have also included the easiest method for making the change from standard to open tuning.

|   | Standard tuning |   |   |   |   |   |   | Open G tuning |   |   |   |   |
|---|---|---|---|---|---|---|---|---|---|---|---|---|
|   | E | A | D | G | B | E |   | D | G | D | G | B | D |
|   | ⑥ | ⑤ | ④ | ③ | ② | ① |   | ⑥ | ⑤ | ④ | ③ | ② | ① |

Tuning to Open G from standard tuning:

1. Tune ⑥ (E) down to match ④ (D), one octave lower.
2. Tune ① (E) down to match ④ (D), one octave higher.
3. Tune ① (A) down to match ③ (G), one octave lower.

As you can see, in Open G tuning, the open strings contain the root (G), 3rd (B), and 5th (D) of a G major triad. This allows you to cover all six strings with the slide, if you so desire. You would not ordinarily do this in standard tuning, as a dissonant, minorish tonality would occur with the inclusion of the flat third.

As you move the slide up and down the neck, a different major triad is created at each fret. In the key of G, for instance, the I chord is located at the nut with the open strings and at the 12th fret; the IV chord is at the 5th fret and the V chord at the 7th fret. If a capo is used to change keys, the I chord, or tonic, would be at whatever fret the capo was placed, while the IV chord would be five frets above the tonic, and the V chord seven frets above.

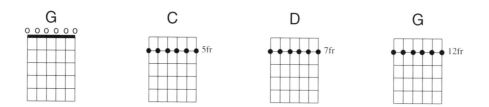

Track 18 is a 12-bar solo blues in Open G tuning. It is a variation on several of Muddy's tunes, including "I Feel Like Going Home." You will notice that the first four bars have a descending double-stop pattern that implies movement from an inverted G7 (F, the ♭7, is on the bottom) to G major. Bars 5 and 6 suggest the IV (C) chord change by isolating the root-fifth (C–G) along with the B♭ (♭7) note. Measure 7 uses a classic three-note form at the 12th fret for the G chord. Bar 8 offers resolution to the G7 chord, which in turn leads us to the V chord in bar 9. The turnaround starting in bar 9 is frequently used in Open G as it lays nicely under the fingers and has a full, ringing sound. You can look forward to the next section of this book for a further discussion on open-tuned slide in Elmore James's music.

Open G tuning:
(low to high) D–G–D–G–B–D

**Moderately** ♩ = 72

*Elmore James receiving welcome support in holding up his modified Harmony Sovereign.*

*(Photo:Jim O'Neal)*

# ELMORE JAMES

**H**ad Robert Johnson lived to play electric guitar, he may well have sounded like slide meister Elmore James. As the spiritual and musical heir to the King of the Delta Blues, James became the inspiration for every slide guitarist who has ever heard his bone-rattling blues.

Elmore was born in Richland, Mississippi on January 27, 1918, and died in Chicago, Illinois on May 24, 1963. His mother, Leola Brooks, gave him the surname of his stepfather, Joe Willie James. His was the typical upbringing for a black child in the prewar South, with frequent relocations to various plantations and the deprivation that goes with rural poverty. As he worked the cotton fields as a young boy, he experimented with the one-string slide, or "diddley bow," nailed to the barn door. When he reached his teens in the early thirties he purchased a $20 National guitar and began the bluesman's apprenticeship of rambling to weekend houseparties, suppers, and the jukes. Around 1934, he teamed up with his cousin, "Homesick James" Williamson, another aspiring bottleneck guitarist. The two taught each other as they jammed their way through the Delta. Feeling the need to stretch, Elmore struck out on his own for awhile, occasionally hooking up with his adopted brother, Robert, on rhythm guitar. During this time, he also played with Luther and Percy Huff, Arthur "Big Boy" Crudup, and Johnny Temple. Temple was one of the early proponents of the boogie bass line, and his recordings would have a profound influence on Robert Johnson. No doubt the association with Temple had the same effect on James, as the moving boogie bass line became the rhythmic underpinning of his music.

In 1937, James hit Greenville, Mississippi, and another chapter in modern blues history began. He met the charismatic Sonny Boy Williamson II (Rice Miller) and Robert Johnson's stepson, Robert Lockwood, Jr., for what would be a lifelong friendship. And, in a stroke of fate, while gigging in the vicinity of towns like Belzoni, Indianola, Leland, and Hollendale, he crossed paths with Mr. Johnson himself in Greenwood. The legendary Johnson's "Dust My Broom" would have such impact on James that it became the predominant sound in his music for the rest of his career.

After Johnson was cut down in 1938, James, discouraged with his lack of success, moved to Jackson to work in his brother Robert's radio shop. Years of scuffling to get by and playing with Sonny Boy followed, interrupted from 1943–45 by an honorable tour of duty overseas in the Navy. He returned to the Delta, reuniting with Sonny Boy, who was now a regular on KFFA's King Biscuit Time show in Helena, Arkansas. In addition to working the joints with Sonny Boy, he travelled north to Memphis to play with Homesick James. By 1948 he, too, was in Helena, broadcasting on KFFA and raising a little sand with "Dust My Broom."

In 1951, independent record producer and furniture dealer, Lillian McMurry, nabbed Sonny Boy to cut some tracks for her Trumpet Records label. Williamson recommended that she record his buddies Willie Love and Elmore. In August 1951, the epochal "Dust My Broom" was committed to vinyl. For someone whose music is so raw and aggressive, Elmore was extremely shy and had to be "tricked" into recording, thinking it was just a rehearsal. Unwilling to come up with another side for his single, James split, breaking his contract and leaving Trumpet to put "Catfish Blues," by the uncredited BoBo Thomas, on the flip side. (James never recorded for Trumpet again, though he called McMurry in 1955 after the Bihari brothers had dumped him, inquiring if she needed a "good artist?" She, of course, replied in the affirmative, but he never showed.) "Dust My Broom" boogied to number nine on the Billboard R&B charts in 1952.

Within a year, he was cutting sides for Joe Bihari's Meteor and Flair labels. He had his second biggest hit, "I Believe," and had settled in Chicago with his band, the Broomdusters. A session with Chess in 1953 yielded "Madison Blues," "Whose Muddy Shoes," and "My Best Friend," but stardom on the order of Muddy and Wolf did not materialize, and it would be 1960 before he would record for Chess again.

During the fifties, James shuttled back and forth between Chicago and Mississippi. His always reliable sidemen included Ike Turner, Johnny Jones, and Big Moose Walker (piano), Sonny Boy Williamson II (harp), Homesick James, Wayne Bennett, and Eddie Taylor (guitar), Ransom Knowling and Willie Dixon (bass), and Odie Payne (drums). Besides recording for the Modern and Chief labels, he backed Big Joe Turner, Junior Wells, J.T. Brown, and Johnny Jones. As popular as he was with steady record sales, existence for the road-weary bluesman was always precarious even as he dealt with poor health and a string of "marriages." By 1957, changing musical tastes had forced him back to the grinding Chicago club scene. In 1958, he briefly took a job as a DJ in Jackson, Mississippi, while managing to make regular forays into the studio.

1959 was yet another turning point for James when New Yorker Bobby Robinson of Fire Records sought him out in Chicago. A professional relationship resulted that would last until 1962, when Elmore left Chicago due to a dispute with the musician's union that left him sick and tired and unable to work union jobs. The Robinson years produced a number of exciting and high quality recordings such as "Twelve Year Old Boy" and "Something Inside Me." Despite cleaner production values, Elmore's intensity is undiminished and the musicianship is high caliber, with top New York R&B session men adding sympathetic support. The royalties from these dates helped to keep James afloat.

In 1963, Elmore was called back to Chicago, his union problems were resolved, and a recording session was set for Friday, May 24. He never made what was supposed to be his comeback date, though, succumbing at last to his chronic heart condition with a fatal attack while preparing to go to the studio.

Nervous and withdrawn off-stage, Elmore James blazed like a shooting star in the spotlight. The urgency of his anguished, impassioned vocals and the brilliance of his whipsaw slide are unsurpassed.

# SELECTED DISCOGRAPHY

- *Screamin' Blues*—Pickwick International HHP 5014
- *Elmore James and His Broomdusters*—Ace CH 31
- *The Original Meteor & Flair Sides*—Ace CH 112
- *Come Go With Me*—Charly R&B CRB 1212
- *To Know a Man*—Impact Records IMDLP 5.00028 M
- *Whose Muddy Shoes* (with John Brim)—Chess CH 9114

(NOTE: Elmore's recordings have been issued and reissued on many different labels over the years, with much duplication.)

# OPEN D TUNING

Elmore James played almost exclusively in Open D tuning. This tuning is the most natural for guitarists used to standard tuning. As opposed to Open G, Open D is based on the E-form barre chord, generally agreed to be the easiest to move up and down the neck as both E strings contain the root.

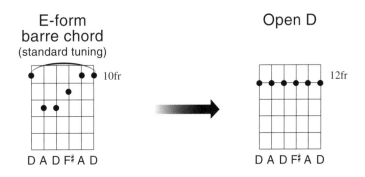

Below are the open strings in standard tuning (low to high) alongside the open strings in Open D, followed by the easiest method for making the change from standard to open tuning:

| Standard tuning | | | | | | Open D tuning | | | | | |
|---|---|---|---|---|---|---|---|---|---|---|---|
| E | A | D | G | B | E | D | A | D | F♯ | A | D |
| ⑥ | ⑤ | ④ | ③ | ② | ① | ⑥ | ⑤ | ④ | ③ | ② | ① |

Tuning to Open D from standard tuning:

1. Tune ⑥ (E) down to match ④ (D), one octave lower.
2. Tune ① (E) down to match ④ (D), one octave higher.
3. Tune ② (B) down to match ⑤ (A), one octave higher.
4. Tune ③ (G) down to match fret 4, ④ (F♯).

NOTE: As with Open G and standard tuned slide, I recommend wearing the slide on the pinky finger.

Track 19 is based on Elmore's landmark, "Dust My Broom," which was a version of the Robert Johnson original, "I Believe I'll Dust My Broom." Johnson himself was probably inspired by Kokomo Arnold's "Sagefield Woman Blues." This theme was, in all probability, a Delta tradition whose origins have become obscured by the passage of time.

TRACK 19

Open D tuning:
(low to high) D–A–D–F#–A–D

Moderately ♩ = 106

Bars 1, 3, and 7 contain the most imitated (not the least of which by Elmore!) slide lick of all time. Note that it is a first inversion D major triad. I have taken advantage of the ease with which keys can be changed in Open D by moving to G in bars 5, 6, and 10, and A in bars 9 and 12. Elmore actually played his version almost entirely between frets 12 and 15.

Another factor that makes Open D so attractive is the access it affords to the boogie bass line. As you can see in bars 2, 4, and 8, the boogie line in D can be played with the open bass strings and the index finger. In bar 5, the G boogie line is played by barring the 4th and 5th strings with the index finger, and using the third finger to add the alternating VI (E) note.

"It Hurts Me, Too" is the impetus for Track 20. Though the bulk of Elmore's repertoire is comprised of 12-bar progressions, 8-bar structures occur occasionally, with "Goodbye, Baby" being another superb 8-bar blues. As in the previous example, the boogie bass line is inserted between the slide licks to provide the rhythmic and harmonic accompaniment. As you explore other 8-bar blues, you will see that the I–IV changes tend to take place after two bars rather than one or four, as in a 12-bar blues form.

Open D tuning:
(low to high) D–A–D–F♯–A–D

**Moderately** ♩ = 72 (♪♪ = ♪³♪)

TRACK 20

One of the other virtues of Open D tuning is that some blues scale notes can be smoothly inter-grated into the basic chordal slide positions. Note the ♭7 (C) in the pickup before bar 1, the 9th (A) of G in bar 3, and the 9th (E) of D in the bar 7 turnaround. The following diagram shows the common blues scale tones that you can add to form a "slide box."

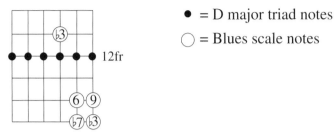

● = D major triad notes

◯ = Blues scale notes

Whether playing in open or standard tuning, string damping is of utmost importance in order to achieve that ringing, singing quality found in the best slide guitarists. When wearing the slide on the pinky, be sure to *lightly* drag the first, second, and third fingers behind the slide on the strings. Keeping these fingers in constant contact with the strings will insure that only the strings you pick will sound, not the others that can be set in motion by the movement of the slide. In addition, keep the heel of your right hand close to the strings by the bridge, so that you can quickly drop it to mute unwanted string vibration.

Experiment with vibrato by varying the length and speed of the sweep. Sliding parallel to the strings instead of swishing back and forth like a windshield wiper will usually produce a more controlled quaver.

Slides, or bottlenecks, come in a variety of materials, each with their own particular sound characteristics. Heavy brass and chrome plated steel will produce a lot of volume, sustain, and edge. It may be too grating on a trebly, highly amplified electric, but will cut like crazy on an acoustic. Glass is usually too light and thin-sounding for acoustics, but smooth and glossy for electrics. Delta slide guitarists often made their slides from the necks of heavy glass wine bottles (hence the term "bottleneck," as a synonym for slide). Thick glass *will* impart a fatter sound. Copper and ceramic slides are also available and may be what work best on your guitar.

# PART TWO: 1952–1962

The fifties were the golden age of Chicago blues. As the big band and swing eras waned, the primacy of the electric guitar as a portable, self-contained rhythm section was certainly one of the reasons for the success of small blues and R&B combos. Ready and waiting to take this exciting new music to its burgeoning urban audience were Chess Records and the other indies: J.O.B. (J.B. Lenoir, Floyd Jones, Sunnyland Slim, Snooky Pryor, Eddie Boyd), Chance (J.B. Hutto, Homesick James), United and its subsidiary States (Robert Nighthawk, Junior Wells, Big Walter Horton), Vee Jay (Jimmy Reed), Parrot (Lenoir, John Brim), and Cobra (Otis Rush, Magic Sam, Buddy Guy).

The decade started out raucous and primal with the electrified country blues of Muddy, Wolf, and Elmore. The rambunctious energy of this music would infuse the rock 'n' roll of Elvis and Chuck Berry as the years passed. Ironically, early rock would borrow the fire from raw country blues and not have its debt acknowledged until the first blues revival in the sixties.

By the end of the fifties, Elmore was dusting his broom for the last time, and Muddy and Wolf had lost a lot of their drive and originality. The future actually lay in the slicker "modern" guitar blues of the Westsiders (see Otis Rush section). Their appropriation of B.B. King's solo-centric style would have the greatest influence on the British blues bands in the sixties, who in turn would focus the spotlight back on B.B., as well as the legendary second generation of electric blues guitarists. Magic Sam, Otis Rush, Buddy Guy, Freddie King, Albert King, and Albert Collins were lionized by John Mayall, Eric Clapton, and Peter Green.

The fifties were also the golden age of American electric guitars. Though innovators like Willie Johnson and Jimmy Rogers began by playing amplified archtop Epiphones and Gretches, the emergence of two new instrument designs would greatly affect how the music was played and heard. The first was the solidbody electric led by Fender's Telecaster (originally called a Broadcaster) in 1950 and Stratocaster in 1954. The high, whining treble of these planks did not immediately appeal to the more conservative acoustic ears of the older musicians. Interestingly enough, however, B.B. King, who is most closely identified with hollow-type guitars, was an early user of the Tele and the Strat. By the mid-fifties, Ike Turner, Otis Rush, and Magic Sam were pictured in publicity photos with sunburst Strats. Buddy Guy would also come to be linked with the futuristic, triple-pickup, whammy-bar weapon. As opposed to country and rock guitarists, the Tele would mainly have Albert Collins and later, Muddy Waters, as its champions.

Gibson's reputation had been built on the Old World craftsmanship found in their superb archtops. Seeing the growing success of Fender's bold new instruments convinced them to release their solidbody Les Paul in 1953. Even though it was unwieldy and heavy compared to the sleek and contoured Fenders, everyone from Muddy to Hubert Sumlin, Freddie King, and many of the Chess sessioneers, got their hands on a Gold Top with P-90's. The fat, brown sound of the Les Paul stood out in stark contrast to the steely bite and snap of the Fenders, though traditional Chicago blues guitarists tend to emphasize the treble frequencies no matter the guitar. The increased power, sustain, and resistance to feedback afforded by the new solidbody guitars furthered the ascendency of the electric guitar as the main rhythm and solo voice in the blues.

The second instrument of note to debut in the fifties was Gibson's semi-hollow ES-335, 345, and 355 series. Combining the warmth and vibrancy of acoustics with the sustain and volume associated with solidbody guitars, the thinlines were a big hit with blues players. With B.B. leading the way, Freddie King, John Lee Hooker, Jimmy Rogers, Eddie Taylor, Jody Williams, Luther Tucker, and, later on, Otis and Buddy, fell in step with the ES guitars. Even today, with the phenomenal popularity of the Strat, they are still considered to be the classic blues guitar.

Gibson, Premier, Gretsch, National, Supro, Danelectro, and Volume-Tone were some of the tube amps rasping away on blues stages and in studios in the fifties. Fender had been a pioneer in the forties, but it was not until the mid to latter part of the decade that tweed Supers, Deluxes, Pros, and the quintessential blues amp, the Bassman, started to make their audacious presence known. The increased volume, harmonic range, and sustain-inducing distortion of the Fenders became the perfect complement to the louder and more assertive solid and semi-hollow guitars finding favor with blues musicians. The substantially greater volume of the new electric instruments would be a factor in leading blues out of the clubs and into the concert halls as it crossed over into popular culture in the sixties.

*Howlin' Wolf at the grand opening of a grocery store with his National.*

Photograph by Ernest C. Withers, West Memphis
Copyright © 1989 Mimosa Records Production, Inc.
All Rights Reserved. Used By Permission.
(Stephen Charles LaVere Archives)

# THE GUITARISTS OF HOWLIN' WOLF— WILLIE JOHNSON & HUBERT SUMLIN

Paraphrasing Shakespeare, Sam Phillips was once quoted thusly, "When I heard Howlin' Wolf... I said, 'This is where the soul of man never dies'." Phillips, the visionary behind Sun Records, with help from talent scout and musician Ike Turner, was cutting sides with local blues and country artists for the Memphis Recording Service in 1951. He would then license the finished product to the larger Indies like Chess in Chicago. In either May or August of that year, "Moanin' at Midnight," with Wolf howling and playing harp, Willie Johnson on ripping electric guitar, and Willie Steele on drums, was recorded. It was the earth-shaking debut of one of the most influential, legendary, and memorable performers in postwar Chicago blues.

Howlin' Wolf was born Chester Arthur Burnett on June 10, 1910, in West Point, Mississippi. He could recall the exact date, January 15, 1928, when his father bought him his first guitar. Tutelage under no less a luminary than Charlie Patton resulted in a rudimentary, but totally effective and authentic grounding in first generation Delta blues guitar. Continuing with the equivalent of a Ph.D. in blues when Sonny Boy Williamson II married Wolf's sister, young Chester cadged harp lessons from the lyrical poet of the mouth organ. Vocally, Wolf listed Tommy Johnson and the white country singer Jimmie Rogers as influences. Musically, he could also point his ham-sized hands at Blind Lemon Jefferson, John Lee "Sonny Boy" Williamson, Robert Johnson, Son House, Lonnie Johnson, Elmore James, Blind Blake, and the Mississippi Sheiks.

A dispute between the Bihari brothers from RPM and Chess, who Wolf was recording for simultaneously, was resolved with Chess securing his services for the remainder of his career and the Biharis getting Rosco Gordon. Throughout the fifties, Wolf's rough and raw Delta boogie blues burst from classics like "How Many More Years," "All Night Boogie (All Night Long)," "I'm the Wolf," "Evil," and "Smokestack Lightnin'." Wolf blew harp, picked rhythm and slide guitars, and roared with Willie Johnson's flat-out guitar in tandem. Additional backing in Memphis was provided by a top-shelf cadre including M.T. Murphy, Pat Hare, and Calvin Newborn on guitars and Ike Turner on piano. When Wolf moved to Chicago in 1954, Hubert Sumlin's wiry and unpredictable guitar excursions would begin to surface as Willie Johnson's role diminished. It would be another half dozen years, however, before Sumlin's light would blaze on Willie Dixon's "Wang Dang Doodle," "Backdoor Man," "Spoonful" (all three with the great Freddie King reportedly riffing), "The Red Rooster," "I Ain't Superstitious," "Three Hundred Pounds of Joy," "Built for Comfort," "Killing Floor," "Louise," and the overlooked "Hidden Charms."

After the versatile and invaluable Willie Johnson departed the studio in 1956, Chess session aces Jody Williams, L.D. McGhee, Lee Cooper, and later, Buddy Guy and Abe and Smokey Smothers, joined the wildly inventive Sumlin in maintaining the six-string powered rhythm section. In addition, some of the baddest Chicago bluesmen comprised the rest of the Chess cast: the magnificent Otis Spann, Hosea Lee Kennard, or Lafayette Leake on piano, Earl Phillips, Fred Below, S.P. Leary, or Sam Lay on drums, and Abb Locke, Adolph "Billy" Duncan, and later, Eddie Shaw on tenor saxophone.

With bassist and composer Willie Dixon's influence expanding, the prominent presence of honking horns squeezed out Wolf's harp even as the guitar section became less dense. Some of the exhuberant spontaneity and abandon that came up the Mississippi on Wolf's broad frame was lost in return for the innovative arrangements necessitated by Dixon's unparalleled songwriting.

Much has been made of the fierce rivalry between Wolf and Muddy Waters. While both men tended to downplay any real friction, there is no doubt that Dixon used their competitiveness as leverage to goad them to excel as he bounced back and forth between them with new material. Wolf was particularly ragged because he felt that Dixon was presenting a roadblock to the promotion of his own skills as a songsmith and that many of Dixon's tunes were inappropriate. Indeed, by 1965 Wolf had stopped howling or playing harp, though the mercurial Sumlin was receiving one showcase after another for his fretboard frolics.

By the time the criminally ill-conceived psychedelic sludge of *The Howlin' Wolf Album* was released in 1969, Wolf's reign had passed. Poor health, poor management, and poor sales of blues singles (Wolf's specialty) contributed to the slow decline. As a testament to the immensity of his constitution, as well as his legendary persona, Wolf continued to perform until 1975, one year before his death from cancer. He died on January 10, 1976 in Hines, Illinois.

Howlin' Wolf was *the* voice of the blues. Outsized and outlandish, he was the griot who perpetuated the link to the genesis of the blues in Charlie Patton and the other Delta monarchs. Like Muddy and Hooker, his blues were the most primal and personal of the postwar era. They live on in everyone who has let them into their hearts and souls.

## SELECTED DISCOGRAPHIES

### Howlin' Wolf
- *Ridin' in the Moonlight*—Ace CH 52
- *Memphis Days Vol. I*—Bear Family BCD 15460
- *More Real Folk Blues*—Chess MCA CH 9279
- *The Chess Box*—Chess MCA CHD3 9332
- *Ain't Gonna Be Your Dog*—Chess MCA CHD2 9349

### Willie Johnson
Willie Johnson is featured on all of Wolf's Memphis recordings and some of the Chess sides up until 1956.

### Hubert Sumlin
Hubert Sumlin is prominent on Wolf's Chess recordings after 1954, with the Chess Box containing his most important work.

- *My Guitar and Me*—Black and Blue 33 548
- *Hubert Sumlin's Blues Party*—Black Top 1036
- *Healing Feeling*—Black Top 1053
- *Heart and Soul*—Blind Pig 73389
- *Hubert Sumlin and Carey Bell*—L+R 42 008
- *Funky Roots*—Vogue 512 503

*Wild Willie Johnson strumming a jazzy A♭6 chord on his funky National guitar along with saxophonist Billy Adolph Duncan.*

*(Early 1950s)*

# WILLIE JOHNSON

English writer Charlie Gillett described Willie Johnson as sounding like "...he was twanging barbed wire with a six-inch nail." On the early fifties RPM recording of "House Rockin' Boogie," Howlin' Wolf exclaims, "Play that guitar, Willie Johnson, 'til it smokes!" Both quotes are accurate introductions to this most ferocious and accomplished electric blues guitarist. He roared right along with Wolf, even as his jazz sensibility encased an iron fist in the velvet glove.

Willie Lee Johnson was born March 4, 1923, in Senatobia, Mississippi. He started out plucking the one-string "diddley bow" nailed upside the barn as did so many of this contemporaries in the rural South. By the late thirties, he was making the house party circuit and around 1941, met Howlin' Wolf in Tunica, Mississippi. Wolf had been gigging with Calvin Newborn, M.T. Murphy, Pat Hare, James Cotton, and Little Jr. Parker. Despite that esteemed company, it was Johnson's suave jazz chords and ice-pick, single-note lines played at speaker-frying levels that would eventually embrace Wolf's howling vocals and eloquent harp work on record. Between their first engagements and Wolf's Memphis debut on "Moanin' at Midnight," Johnson would also play with Newborn, Murphy, Willie Nix, and pianist Willie Love from Sonny Boy's King Biscuit Time band.

Johnson's pairing with Wolf was reportedly in response to the success of the Delta duo of Son House and Willie Brown. The combination of his T-Bone type chording and highly charged soloing with Wolf's gutbucket blues led to a visceral musical tension of aggressive abandon. Apparently, the aural sparks were in some part caused by the tempestuous personal relationship between the two.

Meanwhile, Johnson continued to jam the jukes, socials, barrelhouses, and ball games with his own combo in Mississippi and Tennessee. He also performed as sideman to Parker, Rosco Gordon, Bobby Bland, Elmore James, and Sonny Boy until he packed his grip and guitar for Chicago in 1955. His role as Wolf's right-hand guitar man faded in the Windy City, however, and in 1959, the monumental partnership came to a close. Johnson's talent was not to be denied, though, and he found gainful employment leading his own bands and backing J.T. Brown throughout the sixties and into the seventies. He died February 26, 1995 in Chicago, Illinois.

Willie Johnson is the pivotal guitarist in that space where the swinging, sophisticated, urban blues of T-Bone meets hotly amplified, funky, country blues. Also, he was one of the first electric guitarists to use extreme harmonic tube amp distortion and tremolo to fatten his rhythm work as well as to sustain his solo lines like a saxophone. His recorded legacy reveals him to be one of the most successful and important guitarists in advancing the sound of blues and rock.

# WILLIE JOHNSON INTERVIEW

Noted blues authority Dick Shurman taped an interview with Willie Johnson on July 4, 1970. This excerpt is printed with his kind permission and assistance, and gives us a fascinating glimpse into the blues world of Howlin' Wolf.

*Dick Shurman:* Do you remember how some of Wolf's early songs came about?

*Willie Johnson:* We were riding from Holly Springs, Mississippi… you know, way out east… and I made up "How Many More Years" on the highway. I was hummin' it, and the Wolf said, "Johnson, I think you got something going, let's pull over by that shade tree." So, we pull over, and with all the band in the car, he says, "Hum that again." I said that I couldn't exactly hum it, but that I had an idea, let me get my guitar. So I went and got it and started wailing on it and the cats said, "Wait a minute, I think you got something goin', do that again." So I started playing (sings lick from "How Many More Years") and everybody started to move and rock.

So when we got to the job that night, we said that we're gonna play this number. We were playing at a place called Blackfish Lake, Arkansas. I got my guitar and sat down, and I really cared for this number. Wolf says, "Well, I don't see how you do it." Now, at that time, he couldn't read or write. I went and got a tablet and I printed the number, "How many more years have I got to live on and be your slave?" (Note: This line is different from Chess single 1479, issued in 1951, and appears on an alternate take.)

I printed it down and carried him over it. We played the number and the people were looking at us, not knowing what we were doing! Then when we got back to Memphis, we went to Sam Phillips' Memphis Recording Company… Phillips then referred it to Leonard Chess.

If I couldn't rehearse in my hotel room when we were on the road, I would get my guitar to play in the car while the other folks are sleeping, and get in that groove.

✧      ✧      ✧

# THE GUITAR STYLE OF WILLIE JOHNSON

Track 21 is a I chord country honk that has its roots deep in the earliest Delta blues. As trains figure prominently in the lore and music of rural Southern folk, it is likely that this kind of rhythm derives from the click-clack and rolling thunder of a steam locomotive cutting across the cotton fields.

In contrast to most contemporary blues, which are almost exclusively in 12/8 or 4/4 time, this example is in 2/4 like much country music. The notes are out of the E Mixolydian mode with the addition of the ♭3 (G, in bar 6). Measures 1, 3, 5, and 7 function as the "call" with bars 2, 4, and 6 the "response," not unlike a pre-blues field holler. The partially outlined E7 chord of bars 1, 3, 5, and 7 (as well as the arpeggiated E6 in bar 6) are resolved to a full E9 in bar 8.

One of Willie Johnson's many attributes was his ability to combine jazzy dominant chords with basic blues licks. Like a good short-order cook, he tossed it all together with sizzling distortion, making seemingly disparate elements blend into a satisfying culinary stew for the ear.

This track is in the vein of "Moanin' at Midnight," the Pattonesque "Saddle My Pony," "Mama Died and Left Me," "You Gonna Wreck My Life (No Place to Go)," and "Smokestack Lightnin'." In the sixties, with Hubert Sumlin and an outstanding cast of supporting guitarists, Wolf would occasionally return to one-chord vamps in tunes like "Wang Dang Doodle" and "Mr. Airplane Man."

Track 22 is a 12-bar stomping boogie shuffle redolent of "Mr. Highway Man," "Howlin' Wolf Boogie," and "All Night Boogie (All Night Long)," to name three. Johnson played like a bull in rut on these jumping jaunts, *pounding* out comp cords and molten lead lines.

TRACK 22

*Howlin' Wolf and his band, with Hubert Sumlin playing his Gretsch 6120 Nashville guitar,
June 28, 1968, at the Ash Grove, Los Angeles.*

# HUBERT SUMLIN

As idiosyncratic a blues player who ever bent a G string, Hubert Sumlin has glissed and vibratoed his way to a unique place in electric blues history. Though literally overshadowed by bandleader Howlin' Wolf, relegated to ensemble parts and brief solos, his spontaneity and uninhibited bursts of creativity would inspire other guitarists to push the boundaries of post-T-Bone guitar.

Sumlin was born in that musically fertile region around Greenville, Mississippi, on November 16, 1931. The drums were his first choice at ten, but he switched to guitar a year later when the stomping of foot pedals caused him problems with his feet. As with so many other Delta-born blues musicians, the promise of a better life away from the stultifying drudgery of farm work lured him to pursue a performing career from the age of twelve. After fronting his own little groups, the teenaged Sumlin eventually sided with the even younger harpist James Cotton in the late forties.

Sumlin was aware of Wolf's prowling in the South and had seen him in 1945 and again in 1948. Still too young to legally enter the tavern where Wolf was engaged in West Memphis, Arkansas, Sumlin got his older brother to clear the way with the proprietor for his entrance into the lair. The meeting between the two would be the beginning of a symbiotic musical, but antagonistic personal relationship. Several years would pass before Sumlin was ensconced in the Wolf band, however, and from 1950 to '53 he hooked back up with James Cotton and toured Arkansas and Tennessee.

After the Memphis sessions with Willie Johnson put him in solid with Chess, Wolf moved to Chicago, sending for Johnson and Sumlin to join him around 1954. Though Willie lost his powerful presence on the Southside, Hubert's talent was nurtured as he began the slow transformation into the ultimate Howlin' Wolf sideman. On May 25, 1954, "Evil" and "Baby How Long" signalled his inauspicious Chess debut. The excellent but unsung Jody Williams (b. February 3, 1935) occupied the first guitar chair along with Johnson (until his departure in 1959) and the Smothers brothers, Abe and Otis, through the fifties. Sumlin is the sole guitarist on 1957's "Sittin' on Top of the World," but it would not be until Willie Dixon's tenure as producer, songwriter, and sometime bassist, that his explosive and unpredictable guitar lines would assert themselves. Where Willie Johnson's all-encompassing chordal accompaniment provided a big, fat cushion for Wolf's economical harp solos, Sumlin's wiry leads were the perfect foil for Wolf's howls and hollers even as his harmonica was silenced with Dixon's direction. Nonetheless, from "Howlin' for My Darling" in 1959 to "Built for Comfort" in 1963, Sumlin's guitar breathed with Wolf's voice as an extension of Dixon's vision. This flowering continued on through the late sixties even though the drive and energy diminished, by way of deteriorating health and the ill winds of a changing record business, in Wolf's music.

When Wolf died in 1976, the shy and dependent Sumlin was devastated and stopped playing until 1978, when he joined ex-Wolf tenor man Eddie Shaw's Wolf Gang, playing his familiar sideman role again. In 1982, he finally began his solo career at age fifty, after four years with Shaw. Recordings for Black Top, Blind Pig, and Evidence, along with his emerging vocals, brought Sumlin's broader talents to an enthusiastic blues audience in the eighties and nineties. In 2002, he was diagnosed with lung cancer, had one lung removed, and has been free of the dread disease ever since. *About Them Shoes*, released on Tone-Cool/Artemis in 2005 with an all-star guest line-up supporting, rather than over-shadowing, attests to his continued vigor and vitality.

## THE GUITAR STYLE OF HUBERT SUMLIN

Track 23 is a 24-bar blues in the style of the Wolf's late-fifties, early-sixties tunes that first show-cased Hubert Sumlin's remarkable talent. Though he lacked the muscular rhythm/lead ability of his predecessor, Willie Johnson, and either played straight triads or leads opposite a second guitarist, I have combined the rhythm and lead parts for practical purposes.

Later in the sixties, Sumlin would incorporate wild glisses, heavy vibrato, and unorthodox scale positions in his solos. At the point illustrated here, however, he was using conventional blues boxes, albeit with gusto. While these licks are basic G blues scale in nature, they do show his instinct for dynamic phrasing.

TRACK 23

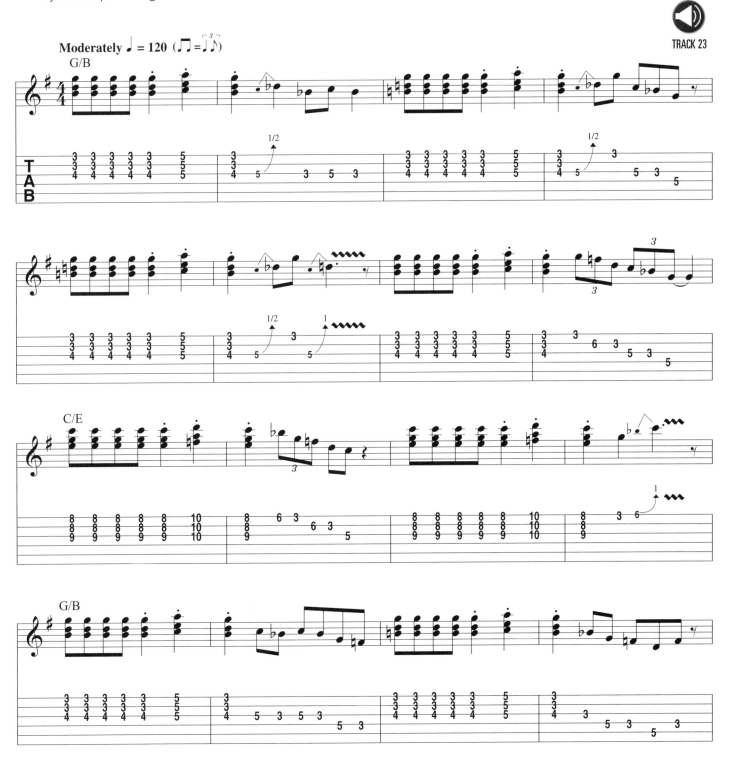

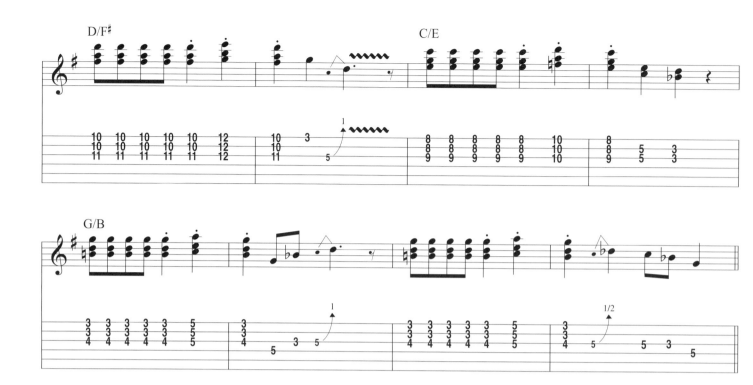

Track 24 is squarely in the realm of "Spoonful," "Wang Dang Doodle," and "Smokestack Lightnin'." Like the first example in Willie Johnson's section, this piece is in 2/4 time and is an 8-bar slice of what would also be a I chord vamp. As in the previous track, it is Sumlin's phrasing that makes this music live. Muddy Waters' description of playing behind the beat, or "delay time," should be your approach to these licks. You should think in terms of an elastic, liquid time—like a heavy weight is being dragged along.

The double stops are in thirds from the E Mixolydian harmonized scale, but note the altered "blues scale" dyad of B/G, with G a minor third. This is common blues practice, with many variations of phrasing and string placement possible.

TRACK 24

*Guitar Slim with his Gibson Gold Top Les Paul (with P-90 pickups).*
*It is rumored that Slim was buried with this guitar.*

*(Photo: Michael Ochs Archives)*

# GUITAR SLIM

The great R&B record producer Jerry Wexler once recalled Guitar Slim's first session for Atco in New Orleans in 1956, "We're waiting in this place for him to come, and he's late. Finally, the word comes that Guitar Slim is on the way. And here comes this entourage of red Cadillacs, people sweeping down the streets, yelling, crazy chicks in red dresses dancing, and then Guitar Slim in all his glory. It is like the arrival of a cardinal or a pope. He comes in, and there's a girl with him, a very pretty girl—she's an exotic dancer. She tells me on the side, 'You gave Slim $2000 to sign up. Well, he picked me up in Vegas and I've been getting that $2000 at the rate of $300 a week.'

The next day we go into the studio. It's hot, it must have been summertime, Ahmet (Ertegun, president of Atlantic Records) and I are dying, but there's Slim with an overcoat on and a headrag and on top of that a fedora, and he's drinking mineral oil—not water—by the pint, to get his voice oiled up!"

Legendary in appearance, performance, and lifestyle, Eddie Lee "Guitar Slim" Jones packed a lot of living into his short thirty-three years. With his hair dyed outrageous colors to match his sharkskin suits, his one-hundred-foot-long guitar cable (to enable him to roam from table to bar to street), his pleading gospel-style vocals, and his loud, emotional solos, Slim thrilled audiences in the fifties. He was one of the archetypes of the shooting star who burns out early, as ten years later Jimi Hendrix would follow in his flamboyant, feedback-drenched footsteps.

Jones was born in mythical Greenwood, Mississippi, on December 10, 1926. As chronicled in his autobiographical song "The Story of My Life" (1954), his mother died and his father walked out when he was a child. Around 1931 he was sent to live with his grandmother on a plantation near Hollandale. Chopping cotton and plowing with mules filled his days with despair, but at night his talent on the dance floor would be displayed at the Harlem Club on the outskirts of Hollandale. It was there, under the lights and adoring gazes of his admirers, that he met Virginia Dumas, whom he married in 1944, when he was eighteen and she was sixteen.

Along with his spectacular dancing ability went a curiosity for the guitar, as Jones would catch Robert Nighthawk at the Harlem Club. He would pester the slide master to let him play, grabbing his guitar between sets and quizzing him on the mysteries of the instrument. Travels with guitarist Johnny Long to see idols like T-Bone Walker and Gatemouth Brown only fueled his passion to play.

From 1944–46, Jones served in the Army, seeing a tour of duty in the Pacific through to the end of World War II. A return to Hollandale after his discharge meant a return to the oppression of farm work. He continued dancing in the evenings, however, and in 1948, at a Delta roadhouse, was spotted by bluesman Willie Warren. Being completely knocked out by the young man's show-stopping antics, Warren sought Jones at his place of employment the next day. He offered him a gig with his band and Jones left immediately to begin dancing for pay. Later he would also sing to the uproarious approval of the Arkansas crowds that were treated to his debut. Warren encouraged Jones to develop his tremendous potential, giving him guitar lessons as well as showmanship tips.

After two happy years on the road together, Jones up and told Warren that he was going to call himself Guitar Slim, go to New Orleans and make records. Arriving in the Crescent City in 1950, Slim scuffled, playing anywhere he could. The mean streets became his stage, and he would serenade his neighbors in the Ninth Ward with rude electric guitar in the wee hours of the morning.

A chance meeting with Huey "Piano" Smith created a lasting musical friendship. Eventually Johnny Vincent, the notorious New Orleans entrepreneur, would become involved in the development of both of their careers. In 1951, though, as Slim was establishing himself on the bruising club scene, he recorded "New Arrival" and "Bad Luck Is on Me" for Imperial. Poor sales resulted in the cutting of his contract, but in 1952 he cut the more promising "Feelin' Sad" b/w "Certainly All" in Nashville for the Bullet label. With a minor hit to his credit, bookings increased for Slim and his band.

In 1953, bassist Lloyd Lambert's orchestra backed Slim, becoming the premier New Orleans band and performing regularly at the famous Dew Drop club. It was here that Specialty Records talent scout, Johnny Vincent, caught up with Slim, wooing him to a contract over Atlantic Records. With another of his piano playing buddies, Ray Charles, added to Lambert's band, Slim cut "The Things I Used to Do" on October 27, 1953. He said that the song came to him in a dream about the devil, and it has been reported that somewhere between thirty and eighty takes were necessary to capture the tune. The stuff of legends, perhaps, but the song hit #1 on Billboard's R&B charts, selling one million platters and becoming the runaway blues hit of 1954. (Note: Jerry Wexler coined the term "rhythm 'n' blues" in 1948 as a substitute for the pejorative "race records" as a way of categorizing black music. Alan Freed, the Cleveland DJ who himself would name "rock 'n' roll," was one of the disc's biggest supporters.)

Though he was no one-hit wonder, Slim never repeated the huge success of "Things." Sellout engagements continued as he toured the nation, tearing it up at the Apollo Theatre in New York and at the Howard Theatre in Washington, D.C. Sagging record receipts caused a split with Specialty in 1956, and Slim signed on with Atco. In an attempt to broaden his appeal in a changing market, Atco turned his guitar down and smoothed out his arrangements with polished studio pros. The original fire of his sound was quelled, but he was actually given more room to solo. He responded with swinging, Texas blues guitar on several "Guitar Slim Boogies" as well as "Quicksand," "My Time Is Expensive," "Down Through the Years," and "Oh Yeah."

The heavy toll of too much wine, women, and revelry came due in 1958. By 1959, while on tour, Slim became so ill that he could no longer ignore his symptoms, and a doctor told him flat out to quit drinking. When the band arrived in New York, Slim had to be carried to his hotel room. When he died on February 7, 1959, his passing was barely acknowledged as the music world was reeling from the deaths of Buddy Holly, Richie Valens, and the Big Bopper on February 3.

Guitar Slim has been unjustly overshadowed by his contemporaries. Perhaps it is the brevity of his eight-year recording career that has perpetuated the slight, but his contribution has been a lasting legacy of tough and tender blues. His singing expressed a vulnerability and secular spirituality that would flower in the Soul music of the sixties. While the swing in his phrasing undoubtedly derived from T-Bone and Gatemouth, the unique rhythms in his solos probably owe much to his dancing days and the prevalent guitar styles of the Gulf Coast. And, like Willie Johnson, he was one of the pioneers of loud distorted guitar on record—to the everlasting gratitute of blues and rock guitarists everywhere.

## SELECTED DISCOGRAPHY

- *The Things I Used to Do*—Ace CHD 110
- *Guitar Slim and Earl King: Battle of the Blues*—Ace CHD 189
- *The Atco Sessions*—Atlantic 81760 1
- *The Things I Used to Do*—Specialty 2120
- *Red Cadillacs and Crazy Chicks*—Sundown 709 08

# THE GUITAR STYLE OF GUITAR SLIM

Guitar Slim could weave magic on slow blues with the intertwining of his sanctified singing and equally voice-like solos and fills. Track 25 is in the style of his slow drag weepers like "The Things I Used to Do" and "You're Gonna Miss Me."

When he rambled to New Orleans, Slim added its unique rhythms to his Delta and Texas roots. One of these funky grooves was based on a 1–3–5 pattern of triads or bass notes that had been popularized in the late forties by the innovative dean of New Orleans piano, Professor Longhair. My arrangement has triadic inversions of the I (F) chord and IV (B♭) chord in imitation of horn voicings. The 1–3–5 melody notes are on the top of each triad. In order to maintain continuity, I have voiced the I7 chord in bars 4 and 8, the IV7 chord in bars 6 and 10, and the V7 chord in bar 9 as three-note, or triple-stop, dominant 7 chords.

Even though Slim played a sparse and basic rhythm accompaniment on record, his horn charts often implied more harmony and movement. The turnaround in bars 11 and 12 reflect this concept with a descending series of triple stops outlining the changes of I–I7–IV7–iv7–VI7–I–♭VI–V7. You should transpose this hip sequence to other keys, making it a prominent feature of your turnaround repertoire.

TRACK 25

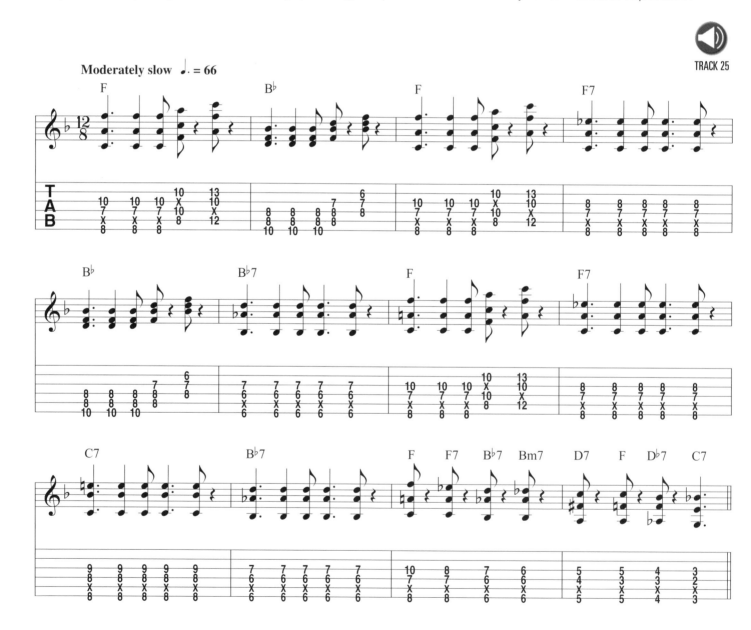

Track 26 examines the Guitar Slim lead method. First, I have diagrammed the major pentatonic scale that he was so fond of. The lack of the ♭3 and ♭7, two notes critical to the styles of most bluesmen, imparts a decidedly major and melodic feel to Slim's single-note lines. Of course, he would augment this scale on occasion with the ♭3 and ♭7, and you should, too.

In Track 26, I have catalogued twelve of Slim's most typical licks according to their chordal function. As you can see from the examples and by listening to the recordings, he got a lot of mileage out of a fairly limited palette of scale tones. It is characteristic of the root, 2nd, 3rd, 5th, and 6th notes to indicate the I, IV, and V chords according to the context in which they are placed. For instance, the 6th acts as the 3rd of the IV chord, while the 2nd becomes the 5th of the V chord. Note the tangy fourths (4 and 12) and thirds (8)—they really add some garlic to the smooth blend of diatonic/pentatonic licks.

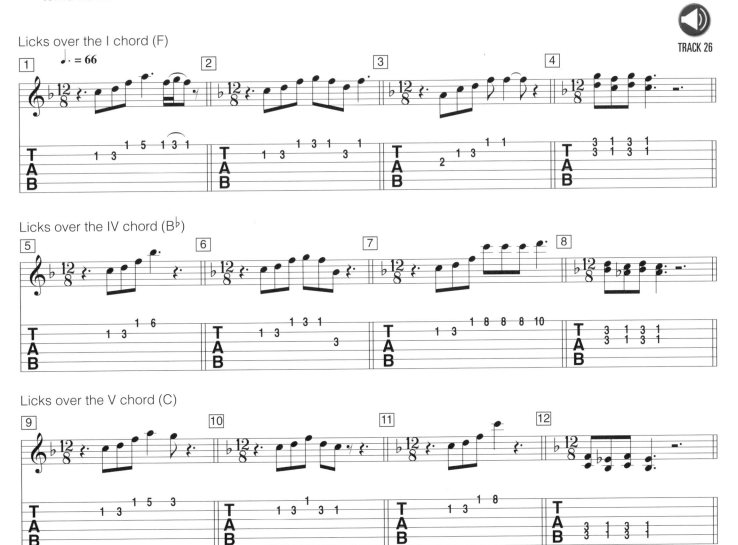

You will notice that Slim did not bend or vibrato much. Along with his running buddy, Johnny "Guitar" Watson, he is one of the few major blues guitarists from the fifties *not* to emulate the fluidity of B.B. King. Perhaps it was his close association with pianists Ray Charles and Huey "Piano" Smith that influenced him to play in a more staccato manner. He did play with sustain, however (in imitation of the sustain pedal on the piano?), as he clipped his tube amps into overdrive.

*B.B. King with "Lucille" (a Gibson ES-355 with stereo and varitone wiring).*

*(Photo: Michael Ochs Archives)*

# B.B. KING

B.B. King is often referred to as the "King of the Blues." Part of it is PR, part is a play on his name. Scholarly types argue whether Charlie Patton or Robert Johnson was "King of the Delta Blues," or if Muddy Waters or Howlin' Wolf was "King of Chicago Blues." These debates make for lively barroom chatter, and they help to keep the names of these legendary performers in the public consciousness. In terms of sheer influence and artistic archievement, however, Riley B. "B.B." King is surely the king of the electric blues guitar. With the previously mentioned exceptions of Guitar Slim and Johnny "Guitar" Watson, no major postwar blues guitarist has established a style without a bend or a vibrato in his direction.

King was born to Albert and Nora Ella on September 16, 1925, in Itta Bena, Mississippi. His mother left his dad when King was four, relocating in Kilmichael to be near her kin. The youngster began singing in the Sanctified Church where his Uncle William Pullian's brother-in-law, Archie Fair, was the preacher. Fair played some guitar and gave the inquisitive child his first lessons. When Nora tragically died in 1935, the ten-year old moved in with his grandmother. During the winter months, after the plantation work had ceased, King attended the Baptist-sponsored Elkhorn School where his strong voice was encouraged in a gospel singing group.

In 1943, he left his family and joined his cousin Birkett Davis in Indianola. To the heart of the Delta, he took his $2.50 guitar and dreams of creating a more ambitious group of singers. In the daylight hours, he labored intensely at plowing, tractor driving, and chopping cotton. In 1944, he received his draft notice, but his plantation boss, with a self-serving eye towards keeping a good hand around, advised him to get married before induction as a way to bolster his chance for an occupational deferment. That same year, he celebrated nuptials with his sweetheart, Martha Denton, scored the deferment, and remained down on the farm.

All the while, King had been picking and singing gospel music with his quartet. Saturday nights were reserved for the blues as he played his heart out on the streets of Indianola. In addition, he haunted the tap rooms, thrilled by the likes of Sonny Boy Williamson II, Robert Lockwood, Jr., and the jivey Louis Jordan. He also began assembling a massive record collection, which further educated and inspired him. Already his eclectic tastes were being developed as Blind Lemon Jefferson and the jazz pioneer Charlie Christian shared time on his Victrola. As with so many others of his generation, King saw music as the path off the plantation. But he could not convince his "St. John's Gospel Singers" to leave Indianola for the more lucrative environs of the big city. Finally, in 1946, after waiting out the war years, he headed out Highway 49 for Memphis, Tennessee, with his guitar, his friend Walter Kirkpatrick, a couple of bucks, and a plan to find his cousin, bluesman Bukka White.

In Memphis, he found White and a throbbing scene of highly competitive and motivated blues musicians. The infamous Beale Street was rife with sharpshooting guitarists and singers who put a chill on King's brash confidence. Fortunately, White took in his younger cousin, tutoring him in the life and music of the blues. For ten months, King listened long and hard, playing with the rough-dried country blues guitarist at home and jamming on the mean streets with the musicians who flocked to the urban Memphis of the forties. But doubts and frustrations caused him to return to Indianola and his wife in 1947. He continued gigging the blues, though, as gospel music proved to provide fewer opportunities for the striving guitarist. A year later, with a modest grub stake from planting, driving, and busking on the streets, he again hit the bricks for the black music capital in Tennessee.

This time his goal was to locate Sonny Boy II in nearby West Memphis, Arkansas. The maestro of the mouth organ had a daily, fifteen-minute live blues show on KWEM. Sonny Boy gave the extroverted King time to do one song on his program, and the twenty-three year old was an instant hit with the listeners. Williamson then offered up one of his overbooked engagements in West Memphis. The proprietess of Miss Annie's Saloon not only accepted the unknown Mississippi singer for the date, but proffered the possibility of steady employment if he could catch a regular spot for himself on the radio in order to plug her establishment.

With winning determination, King commandeered a ten-minute slot as a singing and playing DJ on the new black Memphis station, WDIA. Once again he was popular with the listening audience, and he was granted a half-hour show called the "Sepia Swing Club." For the first fifteen minutes, he spun platters by the nationally known stars of the day. The last fifteen were reserved for him to perform solo.

As his celebrity status grew, it became apparent that he needed a nickname like the other hip jocks. The "Beale Street Blues Boy" was settled on as a way to connect with the blues avenue. Over time, the moniker was shortened to "Blues Boy King" and then "B.B. King."

King's increased profile in the Memphis area led to expanded bookings and the necessity of procuring a backing band for greater commercial potential. Saxophonist Richard Sanders introduced him around to the local pros, and a loose aggregation was formed around B.B. One of these musicians was John Alexander, a pianist who would blaze and burn out quickly as Johnny Ace in 1954 with the hit "Pledging My Love." B.B.'s raw country meter was often out of sync with his sidemen, but they persevered with him, perhaps realizing that under his bumpkin exterior was a genuine talent that touched people.

In 1949, B.B. had a dream fulfilled. He recorded four sides for the indie Bullet label from Nashville under the auspices of Sam Phillips' Sun Records in Memphis. "Miss Martha King," b/w "When Your Baby Packs Up and Goes" and "Got the Blues" b/w "Take a Swing with Me" show him at an embryonic stage with unpolished vocals and rudimentary T-Bone style guitar. The discs did not chart nationally, but they were good exposure and, most importantly, attracted the attention of the Bihari brothers. Besides their flagship, Modern Records, the brothers eventually increased their holdings to include the RPM, Kent, and Crown labels. In late 1949, B.B. signed with RPM and a year later released "Mistreated Woman," "B.B.'s Boogie," "The Other Night Blues," and "Walkin' and Cryin'." In rapid succession, he also cut "My Baby's Gone," "Don't You Want a Man Like Me," "B.B.'s Blues," "Fine Looking Woman," "A New Way of Driving," and "Questionaire Blues" in 1951. Though still smacking of T-Bone's pervasive influence, glimmers of B.B.'s interest in Lonnie Johnson and Django Reinhardt shine through. The years of hard gospel singing and listening to his idol, Dr. Clayton, were evident in the suave, confident vocals.

The association with the Biharis lasted through 1958 and produced some of the finest classics of modern blues. Ringing and ravishing solos, studded with nuance and invention, as well as exuberantly proclaimed vocals, graced the tracks of his breakthrough "3 O'Clock Blues" (1952) and "My Own Fault, Darling," "You Didn't Want Me," "Woke Up This Morning," "Please Love Me," "You Upset Me, Baby," "Sweet Little Angel," and "Rock Me, Baby." In 1952, B.B. signed on with Don Robey's Buffalo Booking Agency in Houston, Texas. So began his lifelong mission to tour 300 dates a year with the full-blown B.B. King orchestra.

In 1961, he was contracted to ABC-Paramount. The sixties saw him go from the epochal *Live at the Regal*, recorded before an ecstatic black audience in Chicago in 1964 to his first and only national crossover hit, the single "The Thrill Is Gone," in 1970. Exposures at rock venues, like the Fillmores, and praise from guitarists Mike Bloomfield and Eric Clapton, helped to spread his preeminence as the godfather of electric blues and rock. As if further proof of his ability to cross race and generational barriers was needed, in the eighties he recorded the single "When Love Comes to Town" with the Irish rock group, U2. *Riding with the King*, a collaboration with Eric Clapton from 2000, was a #1 blues album and went double platinum.

At eighty, B.B. King is still touring, recording, and making personal appearances in his continuing quest to spread the joy of his blues. He has refined his playing to the point where he can literally say it all with one beautifully bent and vibratoed note. And though he has progressed far beyond his humble beginning in Mississippi, he still exudes the same enthusiasm and sense of dignity that has been a hallmark of his blues for sixty years.

## SELECTED DISCOGRAPHY

- *The Best of B.B. King*—Ace CH 30
- *The Memphis Masters*—Ace CH 50
- *Rock Me, Baby*—Ace CH 119
- *One Nighter Blues*—Ace CHD 201
- *Across the Tracks*—Ace CHD 230
- *Lucille Had a Baby*—Ace CHD 271
- *Lucille*—BGO BGOLP 36
- *The Rarest King*—Blues Boy 301
- *Live at the Regal*—MCA 27006
- *Live and Well*—MCA 27008
- *Completely Well*—MCA 27009
- *B.B. King and Bobby Bland: Together Again*—MCA 27012
- *Blues Is King*—See For Miles SEE 216
- *Spotlight on Lucille*—Ace CDCH 187

## THE GUITAR STYLE OF B.B. KING

B.B. says that he cannot play rhythm, but of course he can, and he does it well. From the beginning of his recording career, though, he has relied on piano players, horn sections, and, eventually, rhythm guitarists to provide his accompaniment. His musical mastery lies in his solos and vocals—both are remarkably expressive of the depth of human emotions.

Before B.B., there were the jazzy, single-note acoustic solos of Lonnie Johnson and Django Reinhardt, and the stinging, swinging electric lines of T-Bone Walker. B.B. added in his own spectacular fluidity, soaring bends, and sensuous vibrato that fused the technical capabilities of the electric guitar in the late forties and early fifties. No other guitarist would have such impact on other players until Jimi Hendrix veered up and away in the sixties with extreme volume and whammy-bar manipulation.

B.B. found that he could sustain notes in a vocal manner, beyond what a cranked amp offered, if he bent and vibratoed his strings. In addition, he also realized that with this approach he could achieve a shimmering sound similar to the bottleneck style of people like his cousin Bukka White.

Cellists, violinists, and classical guitarists had vibratoed notes parallel to the neck long before the advent of the blues. It appears that B.B. was the first to vibrato by pulling and pushing the strings back and forth across the frets. This results in a more vigorous and varied vibrato. Most importantly, it allows vibrato to be added to bends for an even more expressive effect. I suggest watching videos of B.B. to glean the subtleties of his technique, but some basic rules apply and should be observed:

1) Think *wrist* instead of fingers when vibratoing and bending. Try to keep your fingers loosely locked in a graceful arch as your wrist twists, moving your palm and, therefore, your fingers.

2) When vibratoing with your index finger without bending, pull your thumb away from the neck, letting it wave in the air like a counterweight to your index finger. The only two points of contact on the neck should be the tip of your finger on the string and the joint where your index finger meets your palm (this is your pivot point) on the back of the neck.

3) When using the middle or ring fingers (again, without bending), apply a little more finger action while keeping the thumb hooked over the edge of the neck.

4) When using the pinky, pull your thumb away, but let the palm of your hand just below your index finger touch the treble side edge of the neck.

5) Hold your notes a split second before vibratoing to give a more sumptuous, swelling sensation.

6) Always back up the bending finger (middle, ring, or pinky) with the others by placing them next to it along the string. This affords much more control, regardless of string gauge or hand strength.

7) Mike Bloomfield once said that steady, even pressure was the secret to a great vibrato. Who are we to argue? *His* vibrato was fabulous.

As far as blues guitarists go, B.B. is the king of the Mixolydian mode. He also knows all his scales *all* over the fingerboard. Let us take a gander at a flock of B.B.-esque licks in three of his favorite blues box positions.

Track 27 contains twelve licks taken from box #1 of the hybrid blues/Mixolydian mode. As with previous artists, I have categorized them according to chord change. I cannot stress enough how critical this is to your development as a focused, tasty blues guitarist with something to say every time you solo. Though his predecessors, particularly Lonnie Johnson and T-Bone Walker, were adept at following I–IV–V changes with the Mixolydian mode, B.B. has made it an art form. Of course, jazz musicians live and breathe "playing the changes," but many blues players use a more modal (one or more scales to cover a progression or entire song) approach, often with great success. That said, if you want to continually grow as an improvisor, *think chord changes*!

Analyzing each grouping will reveal the 3rd and root over the I chord, the ♭3 (♭7 of IV chord), 4th, and 6th (3rd of IV chord) over the IV chord, and the 4th (♭7 of V chord) and 6th (9th of V chord) over the V chord.

Box #1

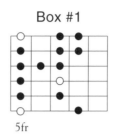

5fr

TRACK 27

## B.B.'s Favorite Box 1 Phrases

Licks over the I chord (A)

Licks over the IV chord (D)

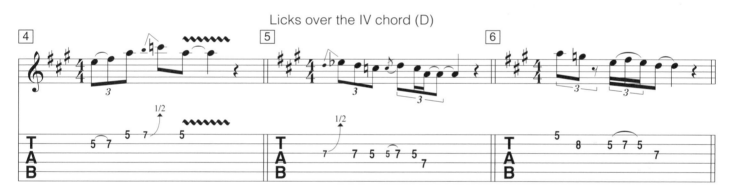

Licks over the V chord (E)

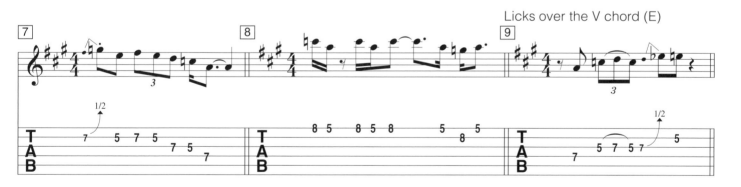

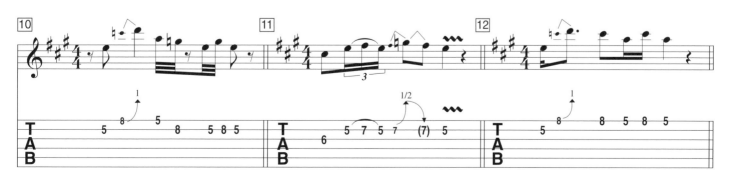

In Track 28 I have notated a typical B.B. King intro from box #1 that incorporates the 2nd and 6th from the Mixolydian mode on the lower strings. Part of the magic of this scale is that a combination of the 5th, 6th, and root notes harmonizes with any of the three chord changes. As you can see from our example, by flatting the 3rd (C♯–C) for the D9 chord, a strong statement of purpose is made concerning the chord change from the I to IV. To firmly resolve the change back to the I (A7) chord, I have used the 3rd (hammered from the ♭3rd) with the 5th, 6th, and root.

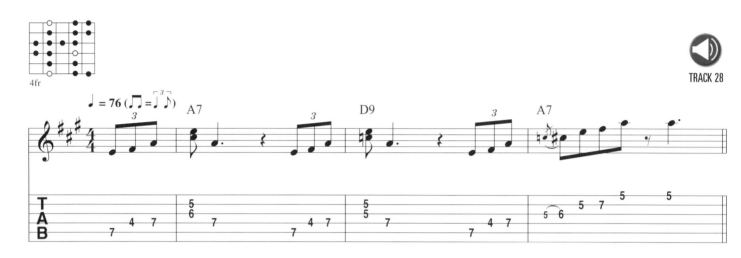

**TRACK 28**

Track 29 has the blues box that is favored by many "modern arpeggio style" guitarists such as Albert and Freddie King, Otis Rush, Albert Collins, Buddy Guy, and Magic Sam. The same basic theories of note selection apply here, as well. Be sure to bend responsibly, nailing a full- or half-step bend accurately. These licks may appear simple, but do not underestimate their power when phrased properly over the correct chord change. Albert King spent the better part of his career in this box!

### B.B.'s Favorite Box 2 Phrases

**TRACK 29**

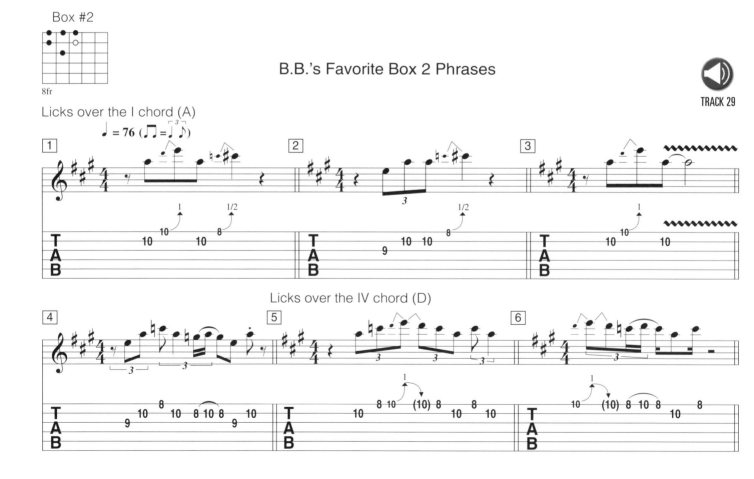

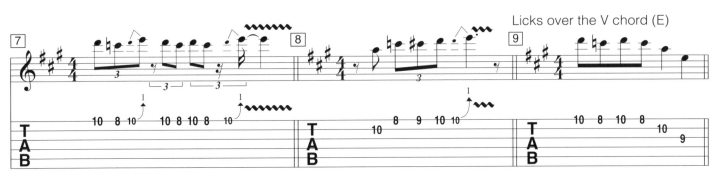

Licks over the V chord (E)

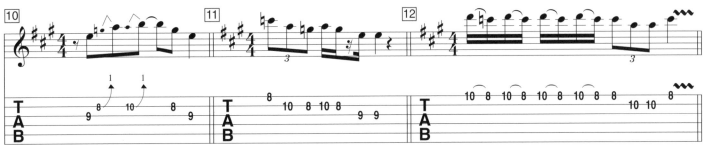

From the sixties on, B.B. has shown such a fondness for box #3 (Track 30) that it has come to be called the "B.B. King box." I think that it must be all that bending *up* to targeted scale tones (another of his innovations) that makes this position so appealing. Accuracy in attaining the exact pitch and fluidity of execution should be uppermost in your mind and hands as you navigate these classic lines. You can achieve B.B.'s cool, slurry sound in licks 1 and 5 if you maintain your pinky on the E note (fret 12, string 1) as you bend, release, and vibrato the B string.

Box #3

10fr

### B.B.'s Favorite Box 3 Phrases

TRACK 30

Licks over the I chord (A)

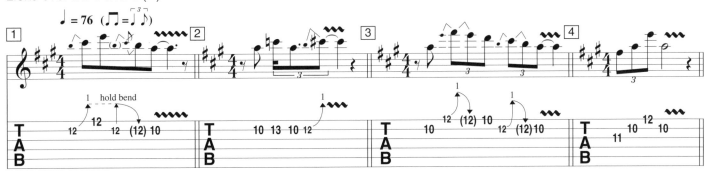

Licks over the IV chord (D)

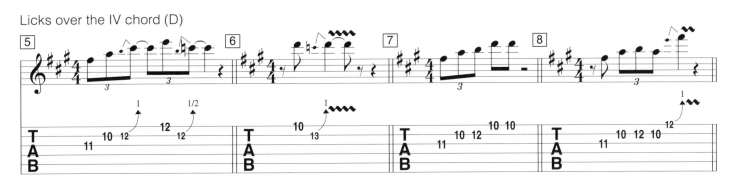

Licks over the V chord (E)

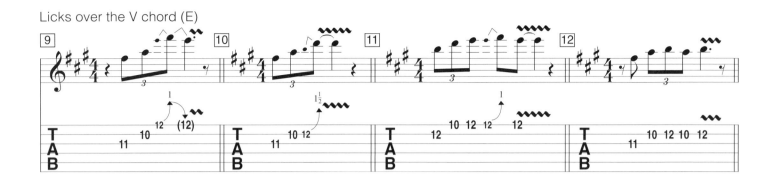

Track 31 is a 12-bar solo similar to B.B.'s mid-fifties Modern recordings like "Ten Long Years," "Crying Won't Help," and "Sweet Little Angel." Notice the repetition of notes in bars 1, 2, 3, 4, 6, 9, and 10. This "stuttering" effect is a great way to build musical tension. You will also see as you play through this piece that it strings together the three blues boxes just covered.

TRACK 31

Track 32 is a 12-bar rhythm pattern based on "Rock Me, Baby." The chords represented here are what a horn section would normally play on this type of number. It is important to make the 4/4 time swing like 12/8. I recommend that you also try playing lead over this track, "soloing à la King" over the changes. Those hip sixth chords should bring out your melodic tendencies.

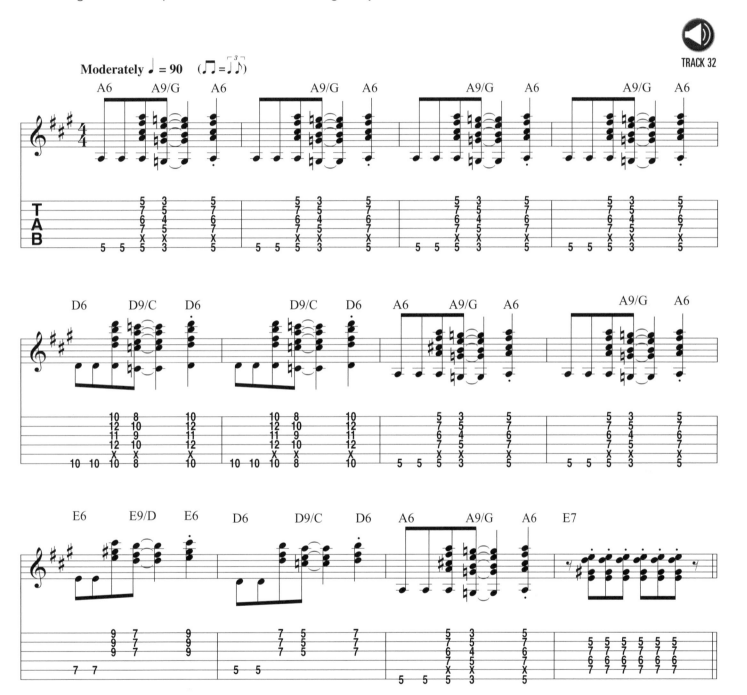

In an anthology such as this, it is impossible to cover a musician as prolific as B.B. King in enough depth. These examples will give you a firm grounding in his style while his recordings, DVDs, and transcription books will further your education on the Beale Street Blues Master.

*Muddy Waters with <u>his</u> Gibson Gold Top Les Paul (with P-90s), left, and Jimmy Rogers, right, with a full-bodied archtop.*

*(Photo: Michael Ochs Archives)*

# MUDDY WATERS & CHICAGO BLUES RHYTHM GUITAR

Though Chicago and Texas electric blues share common roots and characteristics, they diverge in significant ways. Texas musicians were heavily influenced by the territory swing bands that flourished in the Southwest in the thirties and early forties. Horn sections provided the main harmonic ballast, with augmentation by pianos and guitars. By contrast, rhythm guitars were the body and heart of the quintessential Muddy Waters and Howlin' Wolf blues bands. Muddy's band, in particular, served as a fertile environment for the gestation of the "two complementary guitars" concept. The glorious result was the formation of a pulsating web of intertwining parts that set the die for generations of blues and rock bands. The Rolling Stones are only the best example of a group that has built its entire sound around this idea.

Muddy's first sides for Aristocrat Records in the late forties found him playing in a jazzy, swinging manner that was popular in Chicago at that time. His accompaniment usually consisted of piano, sax, and bass. When Leonard Chess felt the primitive power of the hard Delta blues that Muddy was playing in the *clubs,* he acquiesced to Muddy's desire to play the country blues of his heritage. A radical change was effected as the group was pared to a duo, with Big Crawford's doghouse bass as the only other instrumental voice to Muddy's bottleneck guitar. With "Mean Red Spider" in 1948, though, Baby Face Leroy Foster was added as a second guitarist. Foster was better known as an uninhibited singer and drummer, but his rudimentary, chunky comping freed Muddy to fill in more, even as it presented another harmonic layer. Apparently the potential for a bigger, driving sound was not evident to all the participants as Muddy continued to alternate between his duo with Crawford and his trio with Foster. When Little Walter joined in 1950, his virtuosic and innovative harp work contributed another texture and spectacular solos. Not counting the remarkable 1951 recordings of "Honey Bee" and "Still a Fool," on which Walter cranks out telepathically sympathetic second guitar to Muddy, it would not be until the masterful Jimmy Rogers signed on later in the year with "Stuff You Gotta Watch" that the reality of two guitars became, with exceptions, the general rule in the Muddy Waters Band.

Rogers was a pioneering Chicago electric guitarist who is credited with encouraging Muddy to amplify his instrument when they met in the mid-forties. Every bit as sensitive an ensemble player as Walter and pianist Otis Spann, Rogers's nimble fills and chugging boogie lines came to define the *gestalt* of electric Chicago blues through to 1956 when he went solo. His versatility also allowed him to cover the guitar chores by himself as Muddy played little or no guitar on record from 1954 to the early sixties.

Auburn "Pat" Hare grabbed the guitar chair in 1957 upon Rogers's departure. The "Wild Hare" was a demonically aggressive lead guitarist who combined lightning fast runs with razor sharp amp distortion. Picking up where Rogers left off, Hare was the featured guitarist on record, providing tasty double-stop figures and string-torturing solos on "Good News" and "Evil." With "Nineteen Years Old" in 1958, the equally adept Luther Tucker was recruited to join Hare in a blues guitar tandem of electric mayhem. "Close to You" and "Walkin' in the Park" (1958) are two of the finest examples of their fretboard high jinks, with Hare's athletic lead lines and Tucker's bass string licks meshing like well-oiled gears. When the mercurial Hare went to prison for murder in 1963, Tucker moved in on such tunes as "Twenty-Four Hours" with sparkling, vibrant fills and fluid solos. By this time, Muddy's music had evolved (devolved?) away from its country boogie roots to a more "modern," predictable cycle of slow blues and mid-tempo swing shuffles. As such, it was not until around 1964 that the guitar team of Pee Wee Madison and Sammy Lawhorn again continued the two-guitar dialogue. Two other fabulous pickers, Earl Hooker and Buddy Guy, had guested on "You Shook Me" and "The Same Thing," among several others. The Madison/Lawhorn partnership lasted until the seventies when a new generation of blues guitarists, Johnny Winter and "Steady Rollin'" Bob Margolin would authentically recast Muddy's classic guitar ensemble sound.

Track 33 is your average, bare bones, boogie bass line. Though notated as double stops, it is much easier to play if you barre across all six strings with your index finger, using your third and pinky to play the notes on the A string for the I chord as well as the notes on the D string for the IV and V chord changes. That cool embellishment of a ♭3–3 on beat 2 of each measure should be fingered with the pinky.

Track 34 shows the influence that swing jazz from the forties had on Chicago blues in the fifties. I think it may have had something to do with the fact that many of the early electric blues musicians *had* extensive backgrounds in jazz and other forms of popular music. This is straight ahead, "four-on-the-floor" comping with snazzy substitutions. Bar 6 replaces the second measure of the IV7 chord with a minor 6 in a trick taken from the jazz standard "I Got Rhythm." Bar 8 substitutes the diatonic (to the key of F) Am7 for the I, followed by the A♭m7 as a step to the C9 in bar 9. The chromatic C9–C♯9–D9–D♭9–C9 in bars 9 and 10 adds movement and color (the D9 suggests a C6) to what would normally be two bars of the V chord. Ditto for the C9–C♯9–D9–C9 resolution to the V in bar 12.

Jimmy Rogers and the Myers brothers, Louis and Dave, often backed Little Walter with similar progressions. Check out "Last Boogie" and "Fast Boogie" to cop the groove.

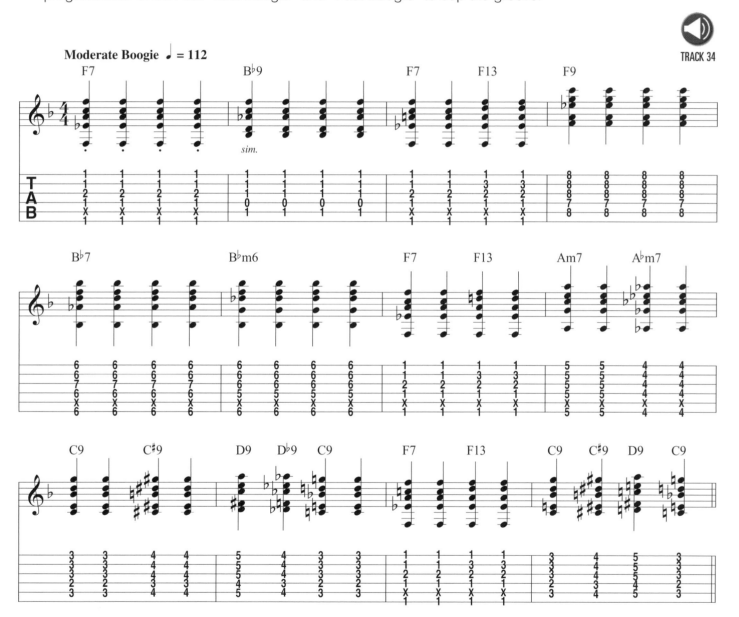

The "Hoochie Coochie Man" and "Mannish Boy" riff is another of those hypnotic Delta blues mantras whose origins are lost to antiquity. Track 35 is a pile-driving variation in open position, in the bluesman's key of E. I like to finger the E chord as if playing a barre chord, with the index finger free. I find that I can then barre the A chord with my third finger. Try it this way rather than using standard "folk guitar" fingerings—it sounds a lot greasier.

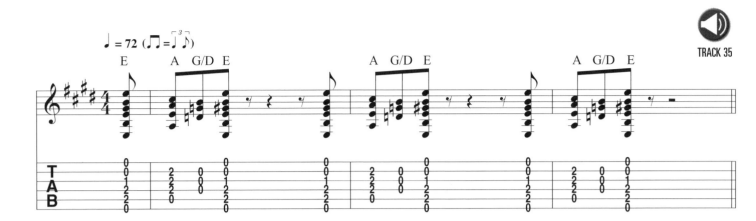

While you are still in the key of E, try Track 36. This 12-bar progression is a harmonization, with chords, of the usual double-stop boogie bass line and is a nifty way to fatten up those generic lines in E and A. In the key of A, just move the pattern played for the A chord up five frets for the D (IV) and seven frets for the E (V). Use turnaround no. 3 (see p. 90) for the last two measures.

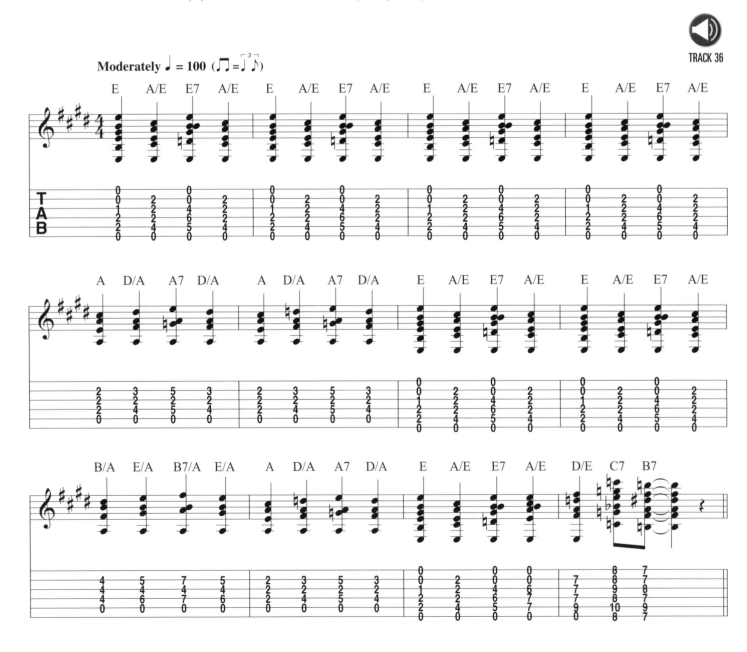

What's that you say? How do you make that progression moveable to *other* keys? Well, one way to do it is shown below. I purposely notated this in F so that you could more easily grasp the concept of moving these patterns up the neck to change keys. I also reduced this example to dyads (double stops) in sixths because I feel it makes for a *bluesier* harmony. You could play this with triadic inversions if you choose—add the third part of the harmony on the string in between the double-stop notes. I will give you a hint to start: add F on the D string at the 3rd fret to the first dyad, the same note for the second dyad, and A on the D string at the 7th fret for the third dyad. The rest is up to you to find.

The turnaround, as you know, is the last two measures of a blues progression. Track 38 displays four common blues turnarounds not covered in any of the previous examples. They are completely moveable to other keys and function well as either lead or rhythm turnarounds. The first note, A, in each turnaround is for illustration purposes only. You could play it on another string, make it into a double stop or even a full major or dominant 7 chord if you wish. The point is that you need the tonic (I) to be sounded on the first beat of bar 11 in a 12-bar blues or bar 7 in an 8-bar blues. More on this later in the book.

## Classic Turnarounds (Key of A)

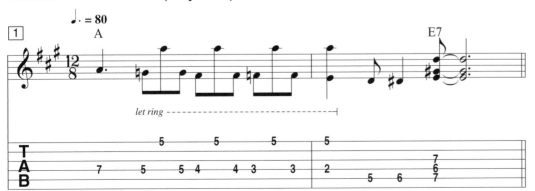

Below are some of the most popular dominant chord voicings used in Chicago blues. Your ear will be the best judge of exactly where to employ them when you are comping behind a singer or instrumentalist. Feel free to experiment with various sequences. Remember, one of the cool things about blues is that you can improvise the *rhythm* as well as the lead.

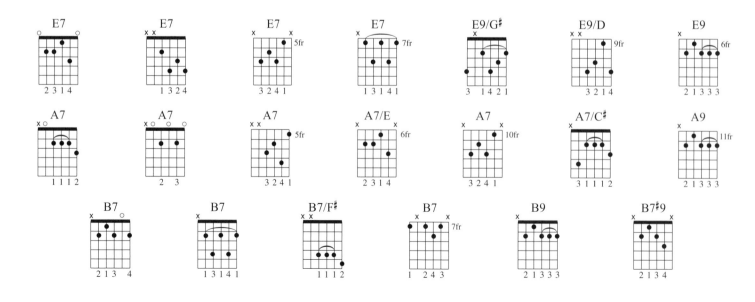

*Otis Rush and his escort, a maple neck Fender Stratocaster.*
*This is probably the stinger that he used to slash his way through the Cobra recordings.*

*(Photo: Michael Ochs Archives)*

# OTIS RUSH

Otis Rush was the most dramatic electric guitarist to come out of Chicago in the fifties. Though heavily influenced by B.B. King, he developed a style based on profound musical statements straight from his heart. Like a saxophone player, he would take a deep breath drawn from his rural roots and then exhale a welter of twisting phrases through his instrument. In between, he sang with a fervor that whispered and screamed the agony and ecstacy of human existence. And though his career suffered more setbacks than most, he remained true to his vision of the blues as his personal story.

Rush was born April 29, 1935, in Neshoba, Mississippi, to O.C. Rush and Julia Boyd. Around ten years old, he began to take an interest in his uncle's guitar. Being left-handed, the young man would flip over the right-handed acoustic and pick it upside down. Later on he would experiment with a standard left-handed model, but like one of his idols, Albert King, he learned to excel at playing backwards.

While still on the farm, he attempted to fashion the requisite baling-wire guitar but soon lost interest. He learned to play the harmonica instead and carried that skill with him when his family migrated to Chicago in 1948. Hearing the seminal Muddy Waters band piqued his desire to want to play blues professionally. Work in the stockyards brought him in contact with a drummer who wanted to form a group, and Rush was pushed closer to giving music a try. Incredibly enough, it was not until 1954 that he began to play the guitar in earnest, with the music of Muddy, Wolf, Jimmy Rogers, John Lee Hooker, B.B., and T-Bone ringing in his ears and rattling off his fingers. In 1955, he played his first gig at the Alibi Club with guitarist "Poor Bob" Woodfork. After scoring steady work as a solo performer, he quit his fairly lucrative warehouse job for the insecure but undeniable lure of the Chicago blues clubs.

Enter Willie Dixon. By the mid-fifties, Dixon was in the midst of one of his frequent disputes with Chess and had decided to work for Eli Toscano and his new indie label, Cobra Records. In his search for talent, Dixon remembered Rush hanging around the Chess studios trying to get signed. After only two years of serious practice, he was good enough to catch Dixon's attention. Toscano, though, was not as astute a jude as Dixon and was unimpressed when taken to see Rush at the 708 Club where he was backed by the Four Aces. As one of the pioneering electric groups, the Aces consisted of Dave and Louis Myers on guitar, drummer Fred Below, and Junior Wells on harp (Wells was usually absent when the Aces backed Rush).

Dixon persevered with Toscano, getting Rush into the primitive Cobra studios with Big Walter Horton (harp), Red Holloway (tenor), Lafayette Leake (piano), Wayne Bennett (guitar), Al Duncan (drums), and Dixon on bass. The first recording for Cobra and Otis Rush was the magnificent "I Can't Quit You, Baby," cut in the summer of 1956 and released as a Top 10 R&B hit in October.

Over the next two years, Rush recorded an amazing string of brutally raw, spontaneous, and powerful electric blues that rival the best of Chess. Included in what would later be referred to as the Westside sound were "My Love Will Never Die," "Groaning the Blues," "Three Times a Fool," "Checking On My Baby," "All Your Love," "Double Trouble," and "Keep On Loving Me, Baby." As opposed to the Southside blues of Muddy and Wolf, the Westside blues performed in the clubs was a stripped-down style that centered around sharp, trebly guitar backed by bass and drums. Jimmy Dawkins recalls that it developed out of economic necessity, as horn sections and other instrumental augmentation was out of the reach of most band leaders. The result was an emphasis on greater musical accomplishment, as the guitar became the main focus for solos and rhythm instead of the harps, horns, and pianos found on the Southside. Other virtuoso guitarists who thrived on the Westside and went on to glory were Magic Sam, Buddy Guy, and, by way of Texas, Freddie King.

When Cobra went under with Toscano in 1959, Rush got his chance with Chess, but his timing was bad. Despite his propensity for creating classics almost every time the tape was running, acknowledged masterpieces like "So Many Roads" (Chess, 1960) got lost in the flurry of activity, and Rush languished for three years. A contract with Duke Records in 1963 led to one single and a growing bitterness and mistrust of the record industry. Regardless of the high artistic achievement of his performances, he did not get to record again until 1969 when Mike Bloomfield and Nick Gravenites produced the ambitious but overdone *Mourning in the Morning* for him. Expectations were high, but the record did not fly.

In 1971, with major bucks from Capitol Records, Rush cut *Right Place, Wrong Time*, what many consider his finest work. Again, fate and circumstances intervened, and the disc was not released until 1976 (with no fanfare) on the indie Bullfrog label. (In 1974, he put to tape the only inferior effort of his career, the abortive *Screamin' and Cryin'* on the French Black and Blue label. Reportedly he was ill and depressed at the time, and the record sounds like it—it is unlistenable.) By then he had moved on, to the infinitely more sympathetic Delmark Records, with the chilling *Cold Day in Hell* in 1975, followed by the live and spectacular *So Many Roads* in 1979. Lost in the shuffle was *Troubles, Troubles*, a beautifully subtle and nuanced recording from 1977 on the European Sonet label (since reissued on Alligator as *Lost in the Blues*).

Several live albums of his recycled standards were released during the eighties as his career stalled. In what can only be called criminally shameful neglect, it took until 1994 for a new recording of fresh material, *Ain't Enough Comin' In* (could his titles be more ironic?) on Mercury.

Throughout his travails, however, Rush never stopped practicing and growing as a musician. A stroke in 2004 has, unfortunately, probably spelled the end of his career. With Buddy as the only serious competition, Otis Rush was the most vital Chicago blues guitarist—the undisputed master of the "singing string," as Jimmie Vaughan so aptly put it. His interest in jazz guitarists, like Kenny Burrell, contributed to his advanced sense of phrasing and blues melody, in addition to a broad chord vocabulary. Finally, the intensity of his bending and vibratoing was challenged only by the naked honesty of his vocals.

## SELECTED DISCOGRAPHY

- *Groaning the Blues*—Flyright LP 560
- *The Final Takes*—Flyright 594
- *Otis Rush and Magic Sam*—Flyright LP 562
- *Albert King and Otis Rush: Door to Door*—Chess 9322
- *Mourning in the Morning*—Atlantic 82367-2
- *Right Place, Wrong Time*—Bullfrog 301
- *Cold Day in Hell*—Delmark DS 638
- *So Many Roads*—Delmark DS 643
- *Lost in the Blues*—Alligator ALCD 4797
- *Tops*—Blind Pig BP 3188
- *Live in Europe*—Evidence ECD 26034 2
- *Ain't Enough Comin' In*—Mercury 314 518 769 4A

### With Others:

- *All for Business* (Jimmy Dawkins)—Delmark DS 634
- *Flimdoozie* (Eddy Clearwater)—Rooster R2622

# THE GUITAR STYLE OF OTIS RUSH

Like Albert King, Otis Rush played left-handed and upside down. The most obvious result of this approach is that he pulled down on the top strings when bending. The increase in available hand strength generates swooping, slithery bends and time-warping vibrato. Though our examples from his early years contain half- and whole-step bends, in live performances, he often pulled the strings a step-and-one-half to two steps or more. He also played long passages on the high E string with a compound series of multi-step and micro-tonal bends. He usually worked out of the first, second, and third blues boxes (see B.B. King section) when executing these maneuvers.

Track 39 is a slow blues solo based on "Checking On My Baby," "I Can't Quit You, Baby," and "Groanin' the Blues." The influence of T-Bone and B.B. can be felt in the G string bends in the pick-up and bars 1, 2, and 6. The first-string bends in bars 4, 5, and 6 are reminiscent of B.B. and Albert King and point the way to the more personal syle that he developed later in his career. There is nothing fancy here scale-wise, just great vocal-like phrasing with pregnant pauses and choice notes. Look how he uses the pickup lick as a theme to introduce the I chord throughout and the IV chord in bar 2. Rush often used motifs as compositional devices, imparting a sense of structure and order to his songs that is unsurpassed by his peers. This quality of "telling a story" instrumentally would have a major effect on Eric Clapton.

The Westsiders were fond of minor key blues, and Track 40 is like three more of his classics. "Double Trouble," "All Your Love," and "My Love Will Never Die" all contain minor triads and their inversions as in our example. I have attempted to convey the drama and dynamics present in the originals. As in the previous solo, Rush sometimes puts rests in the middle two beats of a bar (3, 4, 7, 11, and 12) as a contrast to the tense compression of time in bars 1, 2, 9, and 10 by the triplet triads. As I mentioned, the Westside blues guitarists regularly performed with trios, so these chordal insertions helped to bridge lead and rhythm in their solos.

Track 41 spotlights the melodic sophistication so prevalent in much of Rush's soloing. The four-bar intro owes a big debt to B.B., but the next 12 bars are pure Otis Rush, showing his *stinginess* with notes and his generosity with the use of musical space. Unlike the first example, the thirds and sixths from the Mixolydian mode are drafted to embellish the harmony in the chord changes. Sliding sixths are not a significant element of his style as he employs them sparingly. In measures 1 and 2 of the

12-bar form, they do a great job of emphasizing the I–IV change. After the driving intensity of the triplet triads in the intro, the extreme sparseness heightens the anticipation of the notes to come and isolates, for our inspection, the precision of his note selection. In bars 3 and 7 of the verse, he punctuates the A7 chord change with a pull-off from the suspended 4 to the major 3rd (C#). After giving a preview in bar 4, in bar 5 he suggests the D dominant chord with *one* note, the C (♭7 of D) bent up one-half step from the B. Over the V chord, he teases us by highlighting the D note (♭7 of E) and saving the resolution to the chord's root for beat 3 of the measure. In an impressive compositional display, he brackets the solo with a "rush" of notes in the last two bars, or turnaround.

Listening to "I Wonder Why," "Your Turn to Cry," and "Take a Look Behind" will give you a good idea of what this solo should sound like.

TRACK 41

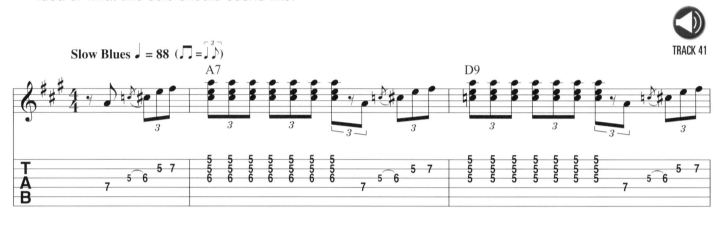

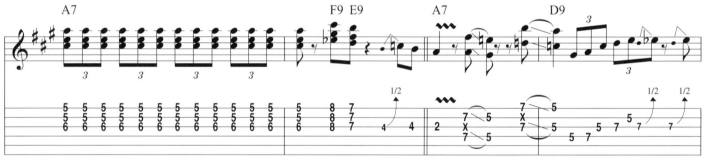

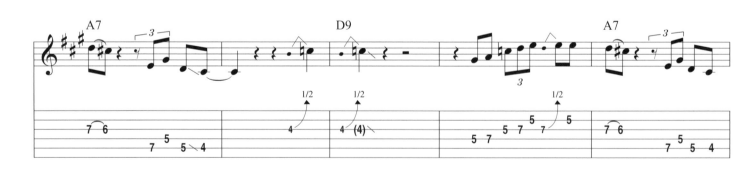

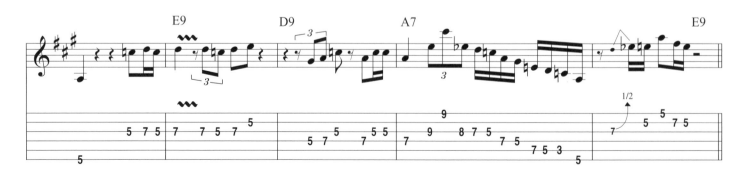

# PART THREE: 1962–1972

The sixties were an era of profound technological and socio-cultural change. In response to the segregation and staid conservatism of the fifties, a revolution was fomented against class, ethnic, and artistic constraints. At the same time, the cold war with the Soviet Union drove science and industry to build up the military and advance the space program. In 1961, man briefly orbited the earth and John F. Kennedy predicted that we would land on the moon by the decade's end. That same year the Bar-Kays, a biracial R&B group from Memphis, released "Last Night," a rocking, blues-based instrumental. In the years that followed, space walks became common while Kennedy's assassination, the struggle for civil rights, plus opposition to the Vietnam War, would help to fund a youth counterculture fueled by the creative flowering of folk, rock, soul, and blues music. In 1969, men walked on the moon, and almost half a million people were enthralled by folk, rock, soul, and blues at Woodstock.

In 1959, Muddy Waters travelled to London with the pride of Chicago blues and turned the buttoned-up British aghast with his amplified volume. It seems the Anglos were expecting *acoustic* blues like Big Bill Broonzy. By 1963, when he returned ready to play his old flat-top in his overalls, the audiences were primed for the unvarnished power of hard electric blues. In the interim, the Beatles, the Yardbirds, and particularly the Rolling Stones had tapped into the vast musical resources of America. In fact, a subculture of English blues musicians including Peter Green, Eric Clapton, Jeff Beck, John Mayall, Alexis Korner, Cyril Davies, T.S. McPhee, and Rod Stewart had sprung up and created a vital underground scene. Riding the striped coattails of the British Invasion of 1964, the blues was introduced to many younger Americans in a roundabout way from across the sea, as groups like the Bluesbreakers, Fleetwood Mac, and Savoy Brown developed a technically proficient and accomplished style of electric blues.

Meanwhile, back on the streets and college campuses of the U.S., blues was crossing over from the farm and ghetto. Besides allowing egress for themselves, white blues musicians kicked down the door for the Kings and their subjects to pass through, and the first blues revival was underway. For the better part of the next ten years, everyone from Mississippi John Hurt to Chuck Berry received the proper respect and (partial) financial renumeration for their tremendous cultural contribution as they performed their magic in clubs, concerts, and at festivals.

With few exceptions, electric blues guitarists in the sixties gravitated away from the big-butt Gibson, Epiphone, and Gretsh archtops favored by players in the forties and early fifties. One of the main reasons for this shift was the prevalence of higher stage volumes to which the feedback-prone hollowbodies were anathema. Gibson's versatile, thinline, semi-hollow ES 335, 345, and 355 became the choice for the virtuosic and swinging Freddie King. The Fender Stratocaster, with its piercing treble, funky "out-of-phase" tone, and increased sustain, made Buddy Guy's blues scream and moan. More than anyone else, of course, Jimi Hendrix became indelibly linked with the Strat as he explored its myriad tonal colors. Magic Sam also found his true voice on the futuristic Fender, though, like Buddy did with the Gibson and Guild, he toyed with a semi-hollow Epiphone Riviera. Both Albert King and Lonnie Mack, being stoic if not stubborn individuals, opted for the idiosyncratic Gibson Flying V. While their decision was mainly predicated on the striking visual nature of the "V," it is a user friendly axe with excellent sustain and punchy tone. Kenny Burrell and his fellow jazzers remained true to the sumptuous Gibson Super 400 and L5.

After an initial fascination with the rich, full tone of the Les Paul in the fifties, most Chicago bluesmen moved on to the thin Gibsons and Fenders. By the mid-sixties, the desire for a lighter guitar with a brighter sound had relegated the LP to pawnshop windows where $150 price tags dangled from their tuners. Then Michael Bloomfield and his singing tone in the U.S. and Eric Clapton in the U.K.

started playing late-fifties, sunburst Standards, and a remarkable event occurred: because of their emerging status as guitar heros, players hip to their sound began purchasing the Pauls in such quantities that the price shot up to $700-$800 almost overnight. It suddenly became very cool to play used, or *vintage* American guitars from the fifties, and a new antiques market was born. The escalating value of the 1958-60 sunburst Les Pauls has continued unabated, with mint examples bringing $150,000! Though blues guitarists were largely unaffected, Clapton's combination of a Les Paul and Marshall amplifer changed the sound of rock into the seventies and experienced a rebirth in the nineties.

Fender amplifiers were the most popular blues amps in the sixties, especially after the introduction of combos with built-in reverb. The Vibroverb was the first such unit in 1963, followed in short order by the Deluxe Reverb, Super Reverb, and Twin Reverb. The Twin, with 80 watts (later pumped up to 100 watts and beyond) and two 12-inch Jensen or JBL speakers, went on to become *the* standard club amp for blues, as well as rock, jazz, and country.

*A proud son of Texas, Freddie King, wearing his Gibson ES-345 over one shoulder like the <u>bad</u> guitar slinger that he was.*

(Photo: Michael Ochs Archives)

# FREDDIE KING

**F**reddie King was the most brilliant post-B.B. King electric blues guitarist. In contrast to his esteemed contemporaries, Freddie was a triple-threat musician—he could play, write, and sing with equal facility. He had virtuosic, fret-bending chops that were always at the service of his songs and a style that was a perfect combination of Texas swing and Chicago grit. His legacy as a player and songwriter exists undiminished, nearly three decades after his premature death.

The "Texas Cannonball" was born to J.T. Christian and Ella Mae King in Gilmer, Texas, on September 3, 1934. His uncle Leon King and his mother were both guitarists, and apparently his mother had the biggest influence on Freddie. He began picking at six on a Silvertone acoustic, but it was not long before the amplifed rave-ups of T-Bone grabbed his attention. As a young teen, the further electric adventures of Muddy and John Lee Hooker would really put the fire in him to play wired up. He also spent time listening to Louis Jordan in the forties, and the jumping and jiving saxophonist would have a major effect on his phrasing.

Around 1950, he made his first sojourn to Chicago, and by 1952, he was a resident of the Southside in search of his hero, Muddy Waters. He not only met the Big Mojo, but Jimmy Rogers as well. It was Rogers, along with Eddie Taylor, who convinced Freddie to lose the flatpick and try fingerpicks instead. The use of a metal index fingerpick and a plastic thumbpick would help define the hard and piercing attack so prevalent in his playing. Thirty years later Freddie got a chance to repay the kindness shown him as a newcomer to Chicago when he produced *The Gold-Tailed Bird* in 1972 for Rogers on Shelter Records.

A meeting with a young local guitarist, Jimmy Lee Robinson, led to the forming of his first band, the "Every Hour Blues Boys," with Sonny Scott on drums, in 1952. In 1953, both Freddie and Jimmy Lee joined harpster Sonny Cooper's band and cut some sides for the Parrot label.

In 1956, Freddie put out a 45 under his own name for the new and short-lived El-Bee label. With Robert Lockwood, Jr. adding guitar licks, "Country Boy" was a midtempo shuffle, with Margaret Whitfield singing a duet with Freddie. The B side, "That's What You Think," was a frantic boogie number. Both tunes buried his guitar in favor of his assured vocals, with nary a solo. The only hint of things to come was the hooky unison bass/guitar line on the latter, a device that he would repeat with great success on his instrumentals. It is rumored that he also recorded some unissued tracks for Cobra at this time, and his friendship and jam sessions with the Westside cats lend credence to the story.

While the El-Bee record stiffed, it was intriguing enough to A&R man Sonny Thompson to sign Freddie to his Cincinnatti-based King/Federal label in 1960. Thompson would also play piano and share songwriting credits on most of Freddie's recordings with the label. What followed were six years of the smoothest and coolest blues of the sixties. Freddie poured his heart out on "You Know That You Love Me (But You Never Tell Me So)," "You've Got to Love Her With a Feeling," "Have You Ever Loved a Woman," and "Lonesome Whistle Blues." He sang and swung with a nimble gait on "See See, Baby," "I'm Tore Down," and "Takin' Care of Business." If he had only cut vocal blues, the excellence of his performances would make him a shoe-in for the Blues Hall of Fame. But equal time was given in the studio for the creation of a blues instrumental catalog. Surf music was just getting a toehold in the sand on the West Coast in the early sixties and King/Federal's president, Syd Nathan, saw this as a way to market Freddie's "twangy" guitar to the pop audience. While "Surf Monkey"(!) did not cause too much of a ruckus, the monumental "Hideaway" (inspired mainly by a Hound Dog Taylor invention) reached #29 on the Top 40 charts in 1961. A selected list of Freddie's instrumental output would also include "Wash Out," "Heads Up," "San-Ho-Zay," "Onion Rings," "The Sad Nite Owl," "The Stumble," and "Sidetracked." Two of his more obscure songs, however, are among the most awesome in blues guitar history. "Low Tide" is 6:11 of non-stop blues improvisation over a chunky shuffle. Without benefit of even a head to rest through, he forges chorus after chorus of spontaneous riffing. Likewise, "Remington Ride," the old Bob Wills chestnut penned by steel guitarist Herb Remington, glides by at 6:27, as

Freddie alternates the melodic head with pumped-up, high-register, string-choked runs. Even though his ballads always retained a respectful tie to B.B.'s original blueprint, by the time Freddie waxed lyrical and muscular on these instrumental masterpieces in 1963 he had molded his own style.

In 1968, Freddie signed with Atlantic/Cotillion and recorded two soulful and funky albums. *Freddie King Is a Blues Master* and *My Feeling for the Blues* featured King Curtis and the cream of New York's R&B sessionmen but got lost in the rock explosion and the tail end of the first blues revival. Freddie left Cotillion and met Leon Russell. Pianist Russell, who had been an admirer of Freddie's hot guitar style for years, offered him a spot on his Shelter Records roster in 1971. Russell was extremely sympathetic to Freddie's music and provided him with the proper backing to record new material and to promote his vocal ability along with his guitar prowess.

RSO Records became Freddie's last label in 1974, and a series of mostly mediocre albums with inappropriate material followed. One positive note from this period was a friendship with one of his famous disciples, Eric Clapton. Tours together were booked, taking Freddie's still fabulous playing to yet another crossover audience and the recording of a good, posthumously released disc, *Freddie King (1934–1976),* with Clapton on one side. Just when it looked like Freddie's career was entering a new and prosperous phase, he died in Dallas, Texas, on December 28, 1976, at the age of 42.

To the general public, Freddie is the least known blues King next to B.B. and Albert. Guitarists who acquire his best King/Federal and Shelter recordings will be rewarded with some of the most varied and exciting blues guitar ever. His was a blues of fire and ice, exhilaration, fierce pride, and artistic achievement. A physically large man with a gentle soul, he was capable of providing tough musical competition and slyly outwitting guitar slingers who would come gunning for him. As Bob Margolin related, Freddie would always solo last at a jam session. After carefully listening to those who went before him, he would then play in a style completely different from everyone else.

## SELECTED DISCOGRAPHY

- *Freddy King Sings*—Modern Blues Recordings MBLP 722
- *Gives You a Bonanza of Instrumentals*—Crosscut 1010
- *Just Pickin'*—Modern Blues Recordings MB2LP 721
- *17 Original Greatest Hits*—King 5012, Federal CD 1036
- *Freddie King Is a Blues Master*—Cotillion SD 9004
- *My Feeling for the Blues*—Atlantic 40497
- *The Best of Freddie King*—Shelter SH 2140
- *Live at the Texas Opry House*—Collectibles COL CD 5253
- *Rockin' the Blues*—Crosscut 1005
- *Freddie King (1934–1976)*—Polydor 831 8171
- *Live in Antibes, 1974*—French Concerts FCD 111
- *Live in Nancy, 1975 VOL. 1*—French Concerts FCD 126
- *Live in Nancy, 1975 VOL. 2*—French Concerts FCD 129

**With Others:**

- *Gold-Tailed Bird* (Jimmy Rogers)—Shelter (reissued as *Chicago's Jimmy Rogers Sings the Blues*—Shelter SRZ 8016)
- Freddie is reputed to be on "Spoonful" and "Wang Dang Doodle" with his friend Howlin' Wolf.

# THE LEAD GUITAR STYLE OF FREDDIE KING

Freddie King commanded the same scale positions popularized by his vaunted predecessors, T-Bone Walker and B.B. King. Though he would reach all over the fingerboard (including open string positions) during extended improvisations on instrumentals like "Low Tide," he mainly stuck to the first and second blues boxes, with the addition of the 2nd, 3rd, and 6th notes from the Mixolydian mode. His extremely robust attack, time-warp phrasing, and boundless invention with common blues forms made him the first blues guitar virtuoso. Even late in his career, when he came under the influence of excessive note-itis from the rock players that *he* originally inspired, his solos and fills always sounded composed and logical, which is not to say predictable—he had too much musical intelligence for that. In a medium that has always valued feel over technique, King managed to meld the two into a style that satisfies body and soul.

Track 42 is a 12-bar slice of prime Freddie King instrumental. The heads of "San-Ho-Zay" and "Wash Out" exhibit similar licks. Notice the prominent use of the flatted third (B♭ in the key of G). Like his Westside pals, Freddie often played the ♭3 over the I chord as a tangy blues dissonance, with the more harmonious employment of the 3rd and 6th notes (in the key of C) over the IV (C) chord (in bar 5). The dyads in sixths (in bars 9 and 10) are another characteristic of Freddie's instrumental work.

Track 43 bears a passing resemblance to "Onion Rings" and "In the Open." Like this example, the heads of those two beauties had improvised measures alternating with bass lines or chords. The first box of the basic blues scale is the source of the licks in bars 2, 4, and 6. In bar 8, however, a hip C9 blues arpeggio is presented containing the root, 3rd, 5th, ♭7, and 9th notes. Cool! Be cognizant of the eighth-note rests that precede the licks in bars 2, 4, and 6. Coming in on the *off* beat is an honored blues tradition, as it bumps the tempo along. In comparison to almost all of the examples in this book, I have chosen to put an *end* turnaround in bars 11 and 12. Look to see how the 6th is subtly introduced in bar 11—that half step between B♭ (♭7) and A (6) gives a sense of acceleration as the line descends to the 5th (G) in bar 12.

**Moderate Blues** ♩. = 96

With so much attention paid to Freddie's hopping instrumentals, it is easy to overlook the seductive power displayed in his slow blues ballads. Track 44, on first glance, seems to be merely a variation on B.B.'s themes. After all, it has that patented ♭3–3–5–root intro and all that second blues box riffing in bar 4. But wait! Freddie adds his own ferocious spin to the situation. That whiplash bending in bar 4 sounds nothing so much as like a chicken squawking, and it sets up the dramatic rest in bar 5. It is then followed by dizzying, twisting high-tension lines in bars 6 and 7. Bar 8 contains a breathtaking downhill run full of hairpin curves. All of this is prelude, of course, to the rollercoaster runs of bars 9 and 10, swooping down and gliding up to the resolution of the implied I–IV–I–V turnaround. Yeow! Punch the play button on "You've Got to Love Her With a Feeling" and "Have You Ever Loved a Woman" to hear Freddie testify his love and devotion.

Several DVDs are now available of Freddie in concert. Viewing these fascinating documents of the man in action will show you that a lot of his musical power came from the fact that he pressed really *hard* with his fretting hand. Combined with the fingerpicks, this made for a searing, ice-pick-to-the-temple effect!

## FREDDIE KING DOUBLE-STOP STYLE

Aside from being a demon with single-note lines, Freddie had a bluesman's mastery of double stops (dyads) second to none. He mainly deployed them in his instrumentals, and he used Mixolydian mode dyads in sixths almost exclusively. Track 45 shows the E Mixolydian scale harmonized in sixths on four pairs of strings. Examples 1, 2, and 4 are ascending patterns while example 3 descends and overlaps with two of the dyads from example 4. I did this because to run the pattern either ascending or descending *only* on the A and G strings, in the key of E, would necessitate a longer guitar neck! By the way, be aware that no matter where they are positioned on the strings, double stops in sixths imply major and minor tonalities based on the harmonized scale. Space restrictions prevent me from giving you a complete dissertation on the harmonized scale, so I suggest you seek this information in a good theory book or from a private teacher. In any case, you should transpose these scales to every other key to see where you run out of frets and have to shift to a higher or lower pair of strings. Try picking them with your fingers or with your pick and fingers.

TRACK 45

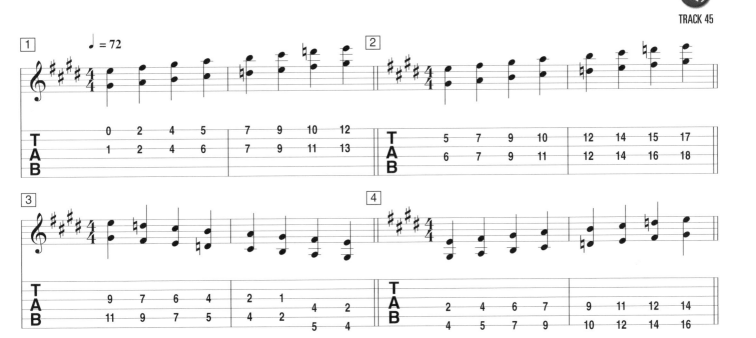

Track 46 shows a typical way to make a I–IV change with Mixolydian dyads. You will notice that in each bar a dyad has been inserted between the 2nd and 3rd degrees that does not naturally occur in the scale. These are *passing* double stops that allow you to have four dyads in each bar, one per beat. In addition, they facilitate the placement of the A/C♯, or root A chord dyad, on the first beat of the A (IV) chord change in bar 2. The effect is similar to a walking bass line where the *root* note is usually played on the first beat of each chord change. You can add a passing dyad between any two that are the same shape, i.e., major (diagonal on strings 1–3 and 2–4, diagonal with a fret in between on strings 3–5 and 4–6) or minor (parallel on strings 1–3 and 2–4 and diagonal on strings 3–5 and 4–6).

TRACK 46

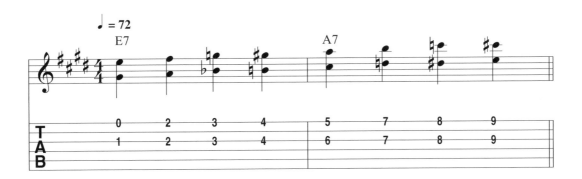

Track 47 is a fragment of a slow, 12-bar blues like "Sad Nite Owl." The half-step movement from the pickup to the first beat of each bar is a form of the passing dyad concept from the previous example. The ease with which dyads in sixths can be slid back and forth gives an organic quality to blues that is one of the primary characteristics of the music.

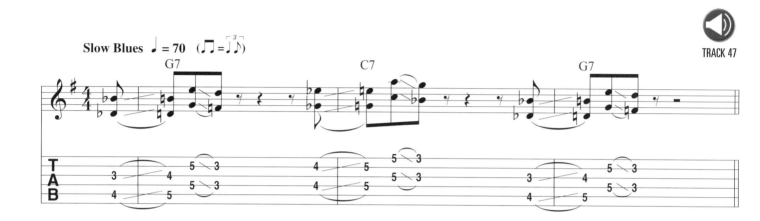

Both "Hideaway" and "The Stumble" contain double-stop patterns in the style of Track 48. In example 1, Freddie takes the liberty of altering the E/G# dyad in open position by making it *minor,* instead of major, as it normally would be. The use of the open G (♭3) string, as opposed to the G# note at fret 1, adds a bluesy dissonance of a ♭3 over the I chord that must have been appealing to Freddie. Perhaps he liked keeping the parallel shape throughout after the major diagonal shape in the beginning of bar 1.

Example 2 sticks to the standard degrees of the E Mixolydian scale, albeit with a dynamic shift in register from fret 7 to fret 4 and back up to fret 12 from fret 1.

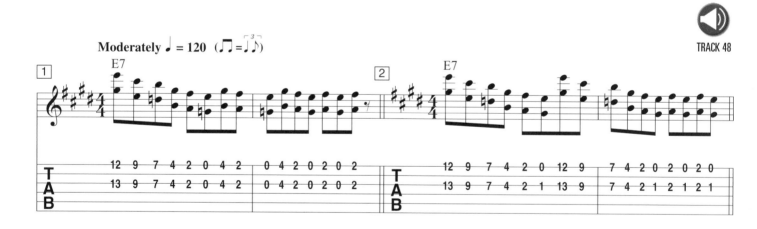

*Big Albert King tweaking the strings on his original issue Gibson Flying V.*

*(Photo: Michael Ochs Archives)*

# ALBERT KING

Albert King, the "Velvet Bulldozer," had the most recognizable guitar voice in the blues. The combination of playing upside down and backwards on a Gibson Flying V, using his big left thumb as a plectrum, and that bending, crushing, caressing touch made a sonic imprint as individual as DNA. B.B. King's solos are extensions of his vocals, his Lucille joining him in harmony. Albert King's Lucy, however, was involved in a passionate and tempestuous relationship with him, shouting and answering back, asserting her independence.

Albert King was born Albert Nelson on April 25, 1923, in Indianola, Mississippi, to Mary Blevins and given the surname of his stepfather, Will Nelson. Though Nelson was a guitarist, Albert was not allowed to play his guitar and fashioned his own "diddley bow" when he was six. Seeing Blind Lemon Jefferson in person around Forest City, Arkansas inspired him to make a cigar box guitar. It is possible that Jefferson's style of accompanying himself with lines and licks rather than chords was an early influence on Albert. Blues singer and guitarist Memphis Minnie also left her mark on the young man as he would sneak in the joints to see her when she came to town.

At 18, Albert bought his first guitar, a Guild acoustic, for $2.00, from a man who needed quick cash for a hot date. Being left-handed and untaught, he tossed it over and began playing the right-handed instrument upside down. Almost from the start, he passed over chord development in favor of single-note soloing, especially after hearing T-Bone Walker in the forties.

While doing construction work around 1950 in the Little Rock and Osceola area, Albert acquired an electric Epiphone guitar and amp. Before long he was gigging country blues with his own band, the "In The Groove Boys." With Albert on guitar, Odell Mitchell on drums, and Eddie Snow on piano, they were good enough to play on radio station KOSE in Osceola. Snow later added another guitarist and singer to the group, eventually recording for Sun Records, but Albert left for South Bend, Indiana, around 1952 and joined a gospel quartet, "The Harmony Kings." He stopped playing guitar for a while, moved to Gary and ended up backing Jimmy Reed on drums. Reed's erratic behavior convinced Albert to make a go of it on his own, and he cut "(Be On Your) Merry Way" b/w "Bad Luck Blues" on the Parrot label in Chicago in 1953. "Murder," "Little Boy Blue," and "Sweet Woman" were also recorded, but languished in the Chess vaults (who had purchased the Parrot catalogue) for decades. The single, though unpolished and showing the influence of Elmore James and Robert Nighthawk (sans the slide), gives a preview of the economical and deliberate phrasing that was to come. It sold well, Albert got shafted financially, and he returned to Arkansas for some more seasoning with the In The Groove Boys.

Around 1956, Albert shifted his home base to St. Louis and gritty East St. Louis. The Missouri metropolis had a modest but vigorous blues scene with people like Little Milton Campbell raising some sand. Albert got a contract with the local Bobbin label in 1959 and, with Ike Turner's production help, recorded a significant body of work through to 1963. Finger-snapping, horn-honking jump blues like "I've Made Nights by Myself," "Let's Have a Natural Ball," and "I Walked All Night Long" spiced up the soulful slow blues of "Don't Throw Your Love on Me So Strong," "Ooh-Ee, Baby," and "Travelin' to California." The talking guitar solos, full of signature bends and phrasing, were much in evidence, as was the big, mellifluous voice. In a hint of what was to follow later in Memphis, "Had You Told It Like It Was" and "Funny Feeling" had a girl chorus cooing along, R&B changes, and proto-soul music arrangements. On top of that, the instrumental "This Morning" echoed and answered the Memphisian Mar-Keys' "Last Night" from 1961.

In 1966, Albert signed on with the Memphis soul music company Stax Records. In a brilliant executive decision, Albert was teamed up with the funky and legendary Booker T. & the MGs. In 1967, the epochal *Born Under a Bad Sign* was released. It was a sensational, classic album of driving 4/4 blues-rock like "Oh, Pretty Woman," "The Hunter," and the title tune. The monumental slow blues of "Personal Manager" and "As the Years Go Passing By," as well as the rhumba blues of "Crosscut Saw," came to define sixties blues. For the next ten years, until Stax went belly-up in the mid-seventies, Albert had a sympathetic home for his music and access to a receptive crossover audience. Albert played the Fillmores, festivals, and rock clubs, giving young fans a taste of the real blues in contrast to all the pseudo, psychedelic blues rampant at the time.

In 1976, he recorded for Utopia Records and, in 1977, tried mightily to overcome the inappropriate pop funk provided him by Tomato Records. His recording career then lay fallow for five years until the more empathetic Fantasy label picked him up from 1983 to 1985. The last years of his life found an embittered Albert King contemptuous of record offers and continuously threatening to retire, another victim of the business of music.

On December 21, 1992, 6'4", 250-pound Albert King died, and a huge presence was whacked out of the blues community. To many guitarists, he had come to symbolize "blues power," and luminaries from Clapton to Hendrix to Stevie Ray Vaughan owed a substantial portion of their blues vocabulary to King Albert. As multi-note shred-fests become the standard for blues guitar in the nineties, it can be refreshing to hear once again the laser focus of Albert's hand-crafted solos. To paraphrase Joe Walsh, "Albert King could blow away most contemporary guitarists with his standby switch on!"

## SELECTED DISCOGRAPHY

- *The Big Blues*—Modern Blues Recordings 723
- *Born Under a Bad Sign*—Atlantic 7723
- *Laundromat Blues*—Edsel 130
- *Live Wire/Blues Power*—Stax 4128
- *Wednesday Night in San Francisco*—Stax MPS 8556
- *Thursday Night In San Francisco*—Stax MPS 8557
- *Years Gone By*—Stax 8522
- *I'll Play the Blues for You*—Stax 8513
- *Blues at Sunrise*—Stax 8546
- *San Francisco '83*—Fantasy 9627
- *I'm In a Phone Booth, Baby*—Fantasy 9633

**With Others:**

- *Door to Door (Albert King & Otis Rush)*—Chess 9322 (contains the first Parrot recordings)
- *AlbertKing/Little Milton*—Stax 4123

# THE GUITAR STYLE OF ALBERT KING

I would only be slightly facetious if I said that Albert King did one thing—he bent strings. Actually he did more than just *bend* strings—he yanked them down with tremendous ferocity and authority, as well as with accurate intonation. In between all that heroic string pulling, he also peeled off glorious bunches of snappy runs, bristling with peppery blue notes. His phrases were so logical and primal that they stay with you long after the torrential downpour of the less inspired.

Albert King employed the unorthodox tuning of B–E–B–E–G#–C# (low to high), which, coupled with his upside-down guitar technique and huge hands, facilitated his ability to create all those crazy bends. Inasmuch as he played almost exclusively on the top three strings (which correspond exactly with those in standard tuning), this altered tuning does not seem to have had much of an effect on his style. Of more concern to us mere mortals, though, is how to recreate those bends of a major third (two whole steps) and a minor third (one-and-a-half steps) by *pushing up* instead of pulling down. Besides having your action high enough so that your fingertips get a good purchase on the strings, may I suggest pushing the string you are bending *under* the others? This way you lessen the tension caused by pushing against the lower strings on the fingerboard. This can be particularly effective on the 1st string if you can manage to push and slide it under the 2nd and 3rd strings. Mike Bloomfield claimed that it was his secret to bending like Albert.

Track 49 is a selection of eight, juicy Albert King-type bends. As you can see, most are in the "Albert King box," or second blues box and are presented for you in standard tuning. These are mainly I chord licks, though lick #2 would sound piquant over the V chord with its ♭3 (F, in the key of D) note. Try bending with your ring finger, reinforced by your middle and index behind it. The half-step bends of lick #3 should be performed with your index finger. Concerning those major third bends, you may, (heh, heh) break some strings while perfecting this technique, so I would recommend keeping extra E strings around.

TRACK 49

## Albert King-type Bends

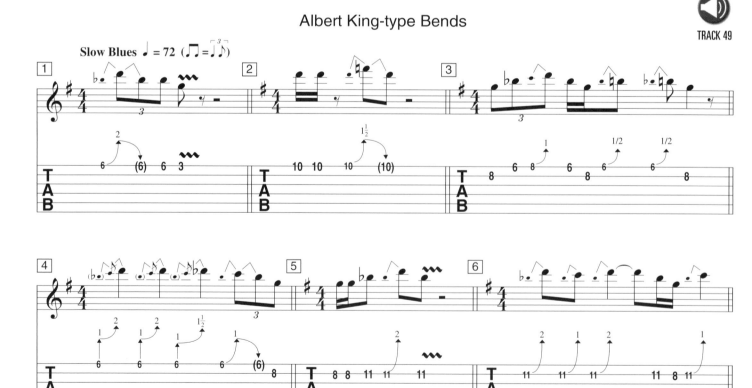

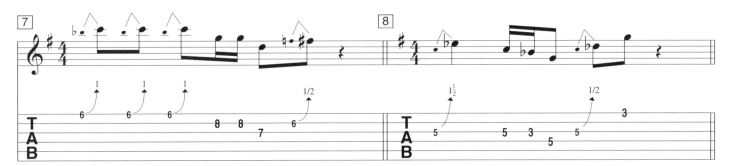

Track 50 is a road map for following the chord changes with Albert. Though many of his licks were interchangeable, make no mistake, he always knew where he was in the progression. As you can see, he emphasized the $\flat$7, 5, and root notes over the I chord; the $\flat$3 and 4 over the IV chord; the 5th over the V chord. Check lick #10 where he plays a triple stop that *implies* a D9 arpeggio over the V chord. This lick could easily be moved down the neck two frets to outline the IV chord, as well.

**TRACK 50**

Licks over the I chord (G)

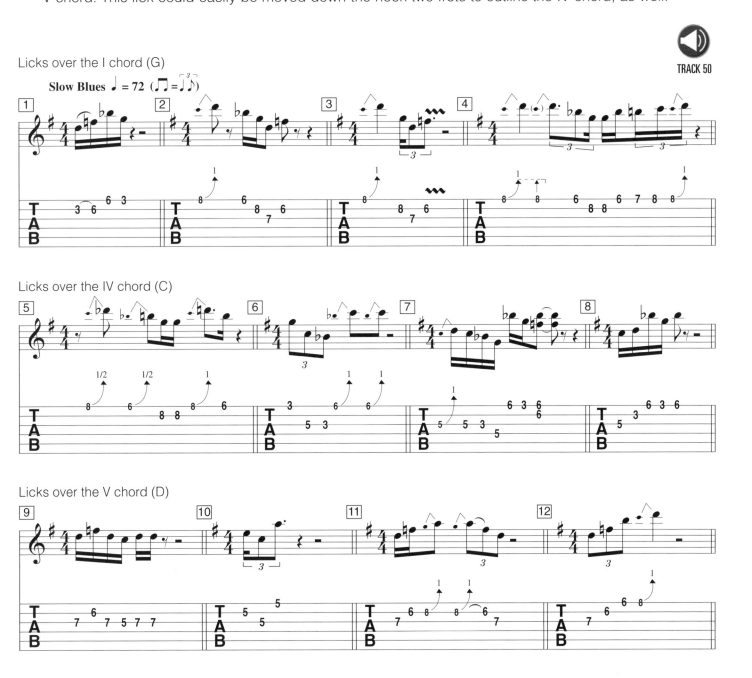

Licks over the IV chord (C)

Licks over the V chord (D)

"Personal Manager," "Don't Throw Your Love on Me So Strong," and "Drowning on Dry Land" are textbooks of modern slow blues guitar. Track 51 is a 12-bar solo akin to Albert's classic ballads. Like his guitar brothers, B.B. and Freddie (no blood relation), Albert had a finely tuned sense of dynamics, musical space, and tension. Be sure to play the bends in bar 4 as such: use your ring finger for the full bends, your middle finger for the first half-step bend, and your index for the second half-step bend.

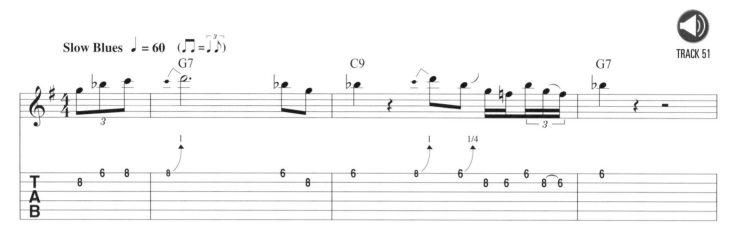

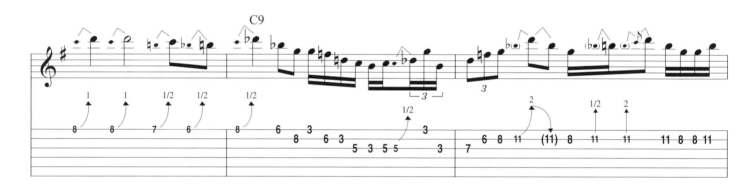

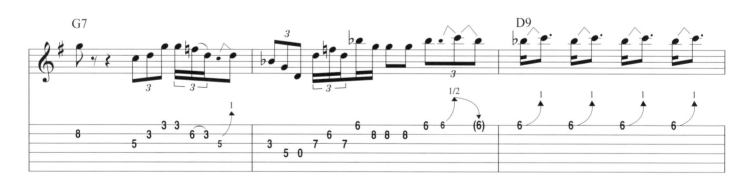

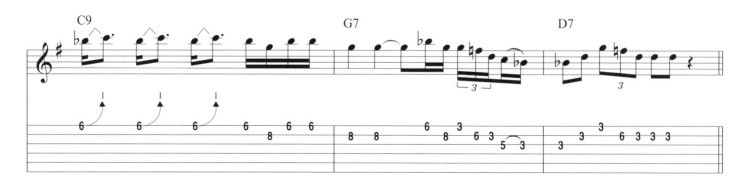

*The magnificent Magic Sam fingerpicking his transition (between Fender and CBS)-era Strat, with rosewood fingerboard.*

*(Photo: Greg Roberts)*

# MAGIC SAM

Magic Sam was the young prince of the Westside as Muddy Waters and Howlin' Wolf were the despotic kings of the Southside. His soaring vocals came straight out of the church while his lyrically propulsive guitar playing represented the sharp, ringing style that he and the second generation of Chicago blues guitarists were taking into the future. His roots were deeply rural, but his heart beat in time to the fast pace of the clamorous urban experience. He preferred to look forward, not back, and his blues reflected the pride espoused in sixties soul music.

Samuel Maghett was born February 14, 1937, in Grenada, Mississippi, to Jessie Maghett and Hetha Anna Henderson. By the age of thirteen, he had quit school to work in the fields and pick his "diddley bow." One of his classmates was Morris "Magic Slim" Holt. "Slim" would reunite with Sam in Chicago where they would gig together and where he continues today to carry the banner for the Westside.

In 1950, the Maghett family joined the northward migration to Chicago. Sam now had a real guitar and played it constantly, even in school where he made a big impression on the girls. Though shy about singing, he became a member of the "Morning View Special" gospel group, all the while avidly soaking up the secular music of Junior Parker, B.B. King, Jimmy Rogers, and Lowell Fulson. In 1954, he formed his first band with guitarist Syl Johnson and bassist Mack Thompson (brothers along with guitarist Jimmy Johnson), and in 1955 they debuted at the 708 Club. Sam's uncle, James D. "Shakey Jake" Harris, had made an introduction to Muddy at the club, and Sam was invited to sit in. The owner was so knocked out that he booked Sam and his group to follow Muddy's engagement.

Sam's brief and sporadic recording career began in 1957 when he put down four taut, sparse tracks for Eli Toscano's Cobra label. "All Your Love" (whose theme Sam would recycle relentlessly), along with "Love Me With a Feeling," "Everything Gonna Be Alright," and "Look Whatcha Done" made some noise in Chicago. In 1958, he returned to Cobra to cut "All Night Long," "All My Whole Life," "Easy, Baby," the C&W spawned "21 Days in Jail," "Magic Rocker," and "Love Me This Way." Tremoloed and vibratoed guitar shimmered over the minor-key ballads and medium shuffles, while the power in his voice threatened just below the surface. It was during the Cobra sessions that Mack Thompson reversed the sound of Sam's name to come up with the hip "Magic Sam."

A disastrous stint in the army, where Sam's sensitive nature responded to the discipline of the service in much the same way that jazz saxophonist Lester Young's had, resulted in six months in the brig in 1959. When he was released after a total of seven months in uniform, his career was derailed and he scuffled locally for the next several years. From 1960–61, he recorded for Mel London's doomed Chief label, followed by two more sessions in 1963 and 1964. By 1966, he had added Crash and Bright Star to his modest resumé. That same year, however, a quick session for Delmark resulted in the recording of the first of his two critically acclaimed albums for the classy new label. *West Side Soul* from 1968 was an emotional and musical tour of Sam's world, brimming with high-energy boogies, minor blues, and a couple of tantalizing soul tunes.

As the tumultuous sixties roared into 1969, it looked like Sam's blues would help to provide the soundtrack. He was booked nationally, was a smash at the Ann Arbor blues festival, and the smoldering *Black Magic* scored as his second Delmark release. Accolades were heaped on this *new* classic of modern blues, and a crossover looked to be in the making.

On December 1, 1969, Magic Sam died tragically of a heart attack at 32 years old. While he had the good fortune to have matured during the sixties blues revival, he did not live to garner the benefits of a long and successful recording career. Nonetheless, his handful of recordings are revered by fans and players alike. His technical limitations stand out when he is compared to Freddie King, Buddy Guy, and Otis Rush, yet his solos burn in the imagination. As a singer, he had few peers and could have had a lucrative commercial career as a soul singer had he pursued it. Best of all, he is remembered as a beautiful and loving man who was happy playing in his living room or at backyard barbecues for his neighbors.

# SELECTED DISCOGRAPHY

- *Easy Baby*—Charly CRB 1108
- *West Side Soul*—Delmark 615
- *Black Magic*—Delmark 620
- *The Magic Sam Legacy*—Delmark 651
- *Magic Sam Live*—Delmark DL 645/646
- *The Late, Great Magic Sam*—L+R 42.014

## With Others:

- *Magic Rocker with Shakey Jake*—Flyright 561
- *Magic Touch/Live at Silvio's* (with Shakey Jake)—Black Magic 9003
- *Magic Sam/Earl Hooker: Calling All Blues*—Charly CRB 1134

# THE GUITAR STYLE OF MAGIC SAM

As the paragon of Westside blues guitar, Magic Sam was particularly enamored with minor-key compositions. These 12-bar progressions tend to fall into three main categories:

1) i–IV7–V7 ("All Your Love," "Easy Baby," "Everything Gonna Be Alright," "Every Night and Every Day," "It's All Your Fault")

2) i–iv7–V7 ("What Have I Done Wrong")

3) i–iv–v ("My Love Will Never Die")

Playing minor blues progressions, even when the IV and/or V chord is dominant, simplifies scale choice. The basic blues scale or minor pentatonic (root–♭3–4–(♭5)–5–♭7) serves the changes well. The ♭3 note functions as the *minor* 3rd of the i chord *and* the ♭7 of the IV chord.

Track 52 is inspired by "Just Got to Know" and "All Your Love." The double stops in bars 1–4 have a nice, bluesy minor feel with the ♭7 (F) note and the ♭3 (B♭). In contrast, bars 7, 8, and 12 of the i chord are built up from the double stops of bars 1-4 and have a more diatonic flavor. These triads can be seen as the first three degrees of the G natural minor harmonized scale *or* the last three degrees of the B♭ relative major scale. Remember, though they suggest chords, double stops are often more ambiguous as to their source scale or chord.

Bars 5 and 6 have arpeggio-like runs based on the C9 chord that really nail the IV dominant chord. Though Sam played basic blues scales most of the time, like all great guitarists he would regularly indicate chord changes and chord quality with exactitude.

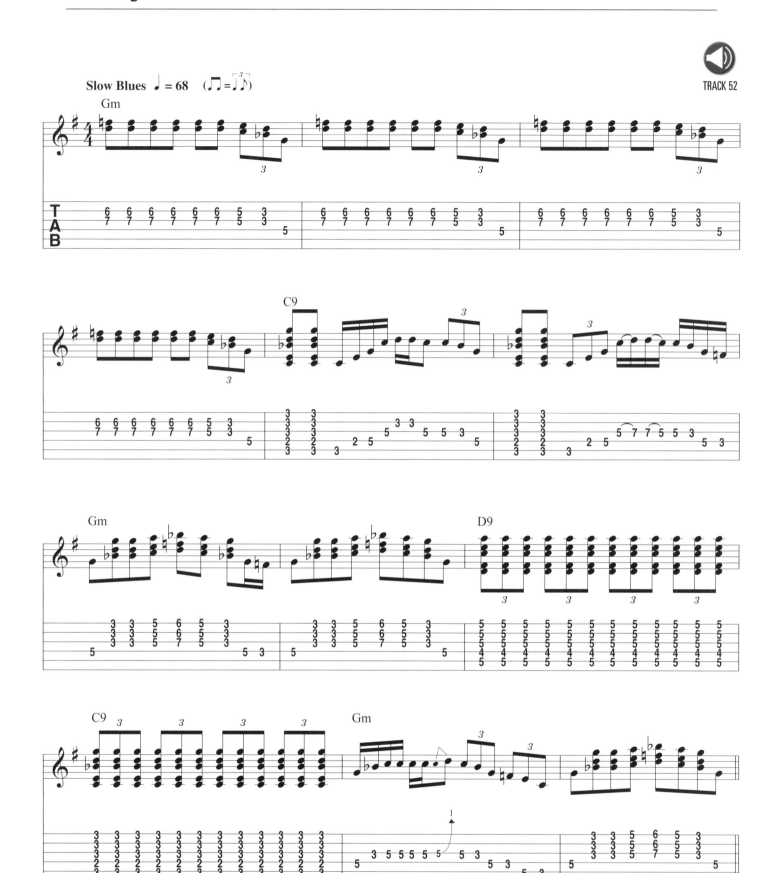

Track 53 is an unusual 12-bar solo consisting of the same three phrases of four bars each. Sam would occasionally employ R&B-type chord progressions such as this in tunes like "Easy, Baby" and "My Love Will Never Die." In yet another characteristic of Westside blues, this solo has structured, repeating measures (1–2, 5–6, and 9–10) played against improvised ones (3–4, 7–8, and 11–12).

Once again notice the liberal use of triads and chords mixed in with single-note licks. Also, the double-stop pattern used for the D9 chord features groovy fourths and thirds that extend the D dominant change with sus4's (G) and ♭9's (E♭). Yeah man, spicy like Sam's barbecue sauce!

TRACK 53

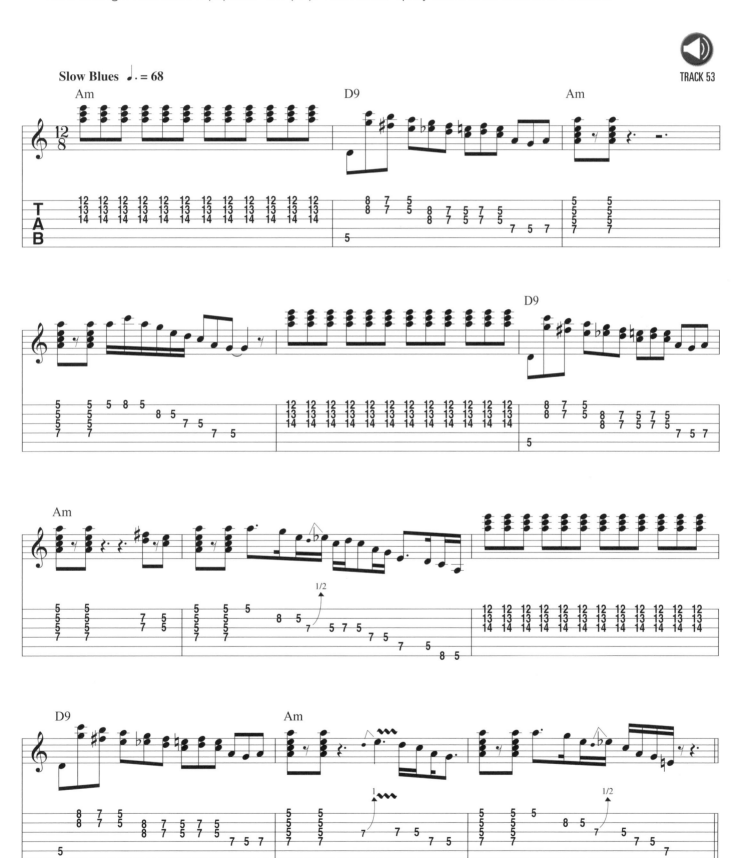

*The volatile Buddy Guy making mischief on a late-model, maple neck Fender Stratocaster.*

*(Photo: © Jon Sievert/Michael Ochs Archives)*

# BUDDY GUY

Buddy Guy uses a rhythm section the way NASA uses Cape Canaveral—as a launching pad from which to send his guitar into sonic orbit. While he sometimes follows the established trajectories of T-Bone Walker and B.B. King, he regularly explores the outer reaches of harmony where no blues guitarist has gone before. Shy and humble offstage, Buddy is wild and uninhibited in performance, singing and playing with explosive energy. Coming out of the same Westside cauldron as Otis Rush and Magic Sam, Buddy has slashed and burned his way to the top of the blues world.

George "Buddy" Guy was born to Isabell Toliver and Sam Guy on July 30, 1936, in Lettsworth, Louisiana. Hearing T-Bone, John Lee Hooker, and, later on, Lightin' Hopkins on the radio inspired him to build his own guitar at thirteen and teach himself to play. His father bought him a cheap instrument when he was seventeen, and he practiced with intensity fueled by the necessity to succeed. Around 1950, Buddy met a singer named Mitchell who provided a new guitar and the chance to play weekend gigs in the Baton Rouge area. Next came an opportunity with local hero John "Big Poppa" Tilley. Buddy's reticence nearly cost him the job, but he persevered and was soon sitting in with Lightnin' Slim, Lazy Lester, and Slim Harpo. In 1957, while contemplating a sojourn to Chicago, Buddy was urged by a DJ in Baton Rouge to make a demo tape to take with him. "The Way You Been Treating Me" and "Baby, Don't You Wanna Come Home" were recorded but not released until Ace Records put them on an anthology called *History of New Orleans Rock N' Roll, Volume One.*

In late 1957, Buddy hopped a Greyhound for Chicago. The competition for work was daunting, but, with encouragement from Muddy Waters, he stuck with it and ended up in saxophonist Rufus Foreman's band for an extended engagement at the Big Squeeze Club and Theresa's. Before long he was haunting the jam sessions, cutting the head of every Windy City axeman who challenged him. At a time when fret-*meisters* such as Freddie King, Otis Rush, and Magic Sam prowled the blues clubs, Buddy's furious fingerboard forays and pleading vocals commanded attention.

Meeting Magic Sam and Otis Rush at a "Battle of the Blues" proved fortuitous. Sam brought Buddy to Eli Toscano and, with Willie Dixon's guidance, "Sit and Cry" and "Try to Quit You" were cut for Cobra's subsidiary, Artistic Records, in 1958. Two more tracks, "You Sure Can't Do It" and "This Is the End," were also put down at a later session with Ike Turner's band backing. Buddy's falsetto screaming and hyper-B.B. King string-choking are stamped all over these initial outings.

When Cobra folded, Buddy moved to Chess in 1960 where he became a house guitarist, playing sideman to everyone from Muddy to Wolf to Sonny Boy II. In between, Buddy got to record intermittently under his own name. These excellent examples of sixties Chicago blues included "First Time I Met the Blues," "I Got My Eyes On You," "Let Me Love You, Baby," "Stone Crazy," and "When My Left Eye Jumps." More importantly for his career, though, the sixties saw the beginning of Buddy's long partnership with blues brother Junior Wells. Starting with the landmark crossover album *Hoodoo Man Blues* in 1965 and *It's My Life, Baby* in 1966, the music from this era is classic Westside blues. Behind Junior's succinct harp and vocals, Buddy comps close-voiced dominant chords, doubles bass lines, and pumps out prickly solos like a consummate trio guitarist.

In the late sixties, Buddy signed with Vanguard Records and put forth three albums of cool blues. *This Is Buddy Guy, Hold That Plane,* and the groundbreaking *A Man and the Blues* proclaimed a mature and confident virtuoso. In contrast to his small club band with Junior, here Buddy fronts a raucous big band, horns bleating in sympathy as his urgent singing sets up his silky, out-of-phase Strat.

Commercial acceptance on the level of Jimi Hendrix—who was influenced by Buddy, as were Stevie Ray Vaughan, Eric Clapton, Jeff Beck, and Jimmy Page—was predicted but never materialized. Though audiences were thrilled with his wanton rave-ups, the record companies did not get it.

Except for the tepid *Buddy Guy and Junior Wells Play the Blues*, produced by Clapton in 1972, Buddy's recording career sagged in the seventies, and the blues community's secret weapon watched from the sidelines.

Finally, in 1981, two outstanding albums were released that represented the next evolutionary step in blues guitar. *Stone Crazy* is almost frightening in its brutal intensity. "Sheets of Sound," a term once applied to John Coltrane's saxophone onslaught, burst from tracks like "I Smell a Rat." This ten-minute opus expresses the rage of a man who thinks he is being cheated on, manifesting itself in an incredibly vicious attack of flesh on strings. As with all his best work, the dramatic use of dynamics, where his voice and guitar careen from a scream to a whisper, makes this cut awesome in its raw, emotional power.

Likewise, *D.J. Play My Blues* showcases blistering guitar antics while highlighting Buddy's reverence for his mentors on the mellow "Dedication to T-Bone Walker." Also in this varied set is the incendiary instrumental shuffle "Just Teasin'." A veritable guitar lesson on tension and release, this tune propels Buddy to use wobbly slurs, severe overbends, whiplash vibrato, and crackling distortion in a dizzying rocket ride of a solo.

Stylistically, T-Bone Walker began the electric blues guitar era in the forties with his "modern arpeggio playing." B.B. King developed fluid string bending and vibrato in the fifties, and Albert King popularized the long, bent-note sustain of the sixties. Johnny Winter brought high-octane Texas blues to arenas in the seventies, while Buddy's "in your face" aural assault forecast the wailing virtuosity propagated by Stevie Ray Vaughan and rock guitarists in the eighties. But, despite the accolades of stars like Stevie and Eric Clapton, the premier power blues guitarist remained without a major label recording until *Damn Right I've Got the Blues* in 1991. With the subsequent *Feels Like Rain* and a string of other albums, Buddy at last received his due from the music industry and the public and remains the reigning potentate of electric blues.

## SELECTED DISCOGRAPHY

- *Buddy Guy*—Chess 9115
- *I Was Walkin' Through the Woods*—Chess 9315
- *A Man and the Blues*—Vanguard 79272
- *This Is Buddy Guy*—Vanguard 79290
- *Hold That Plane*—Vanguard 79323
- *Stone Crazy*—Alligator 4723
- *D.J. Play My Blues*—JSP 1042
- *Damn Right I've Got the Blues*—Silvertone 1462 2 J

### With Junior Wells:

- *Hoodoo Man Blues*—Delmark DS 612
- *It's My Life, Baby*—Vanguard VSD 79231
- *Junior Wells' South Side Blues Jam*—Delmark DS 628
- *Coming at You*—Vanguard VSD 79262

# THE GUITAR STYLE OF BUDDY GUY

When Buddy Guy is in full solo flight, he appears to be operating on pure adrenaline. He knows several of the blues boxes but not the notes on the neck. Be that as it may, he has found a way to tap into his deepest emotions and to express them through his guitar. Also, he is not afraid to make a mistake as his live recordings and performances can attest. In the end, however, it *is* academic. The man plays out on the edge, and if you want to emulate him, you will have to push your own envelope to achieve your goal. In particular, do not be afraid to bend those one-and-a-half and two-step bends *slightly* beyond the target pitch!

Oh well, back to... ahem... academics. Track 54 is an up-tempo shuffle solo that is typical of many of Buddy's tunes, including "Let Me Love You, Baby." It is drawn exclusively from the first and second blues boxes, not unlike the three Kings of the blues. I recommend going over this very slowly as those sixteenth-note triplets in bars 6 and 10 are killers when combined with the eighth-note triplets. When you add in half- and whole-step bends, it can get pretty sticky as the phrasing accelerates and decelerates. For all his note-iness, Buddy is keenly aware of the drama of musical space. What he does best is play in bursts, with the rests heightening the anticipation of what is to come.

TRACK 54

Track 55 is a short 12-bar glimpse into Buddy's high altitude bending style. "I'm Not the Best" is just one song where you would encounter similar licks. He mainly uses his ring finger to bend, backed by the middle and index, shifting hand positions as necessary. No matter what gauge strings you use, following Buddy's example would be "sound" advice. To get that delicious effect on the long, sustained bends in bars 3, 4, 10, and 12, think in terms of *squeezing* the strings, with the strength of your entire hand focusing in on your fingers.

As in the previous example, the use of dynamic space only serves to intensify the jolt produced by the overbending and machine-gun notes.

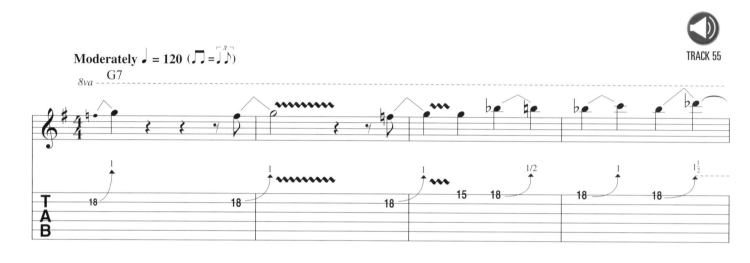

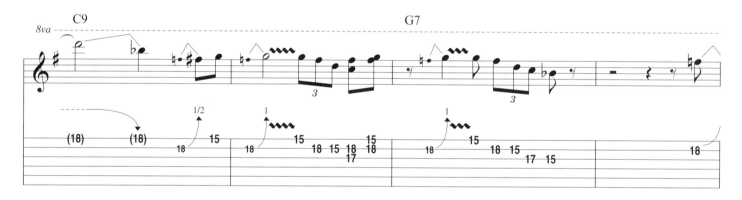

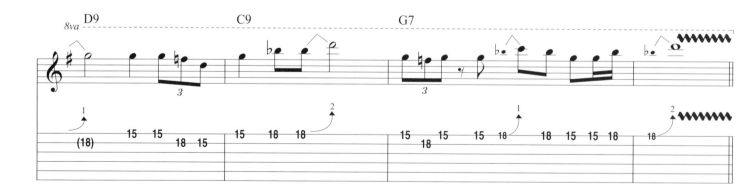

Track 56 is your bonus for trooping through the rigors of tracks 54 and 55. Buddy plays for "the moment" so extensively that he has few patented licks like this one. Theoretically, this is an octave with an inner voice that moves from 3–4–♭5–5. In other words, an octave with a fifth. The fingering is tricky, if not downright difficult. In bars 1-3, start with your pinky on the top note (C on the high E string) and your index finger on the C note an octave below on the G string. Either with a combination of pick and fingers, or fingers alone, strike the octave Cs while playing the notes on the B string with your ring finger. In bar 4, strike all three strings at once while simultaneously sliding your ring finger from fret 7 to fret 8. This can be a tendon stretcher, even this high on the neck, so take it easy. Stay with it though, as this lick offers a refreshing contrast to all that thrashing around in the blues scale. And it gives you time to think about what your next musical idea should be!

**TRACK 56**

# ROCKIN' THE BLUES— LONNIE MACK & MICHAEL BLOOMFIELD

The sixties saw a phenomenon that first generation electric bluesmen like Muddy Waters could not have imagined in the forties—white guitarists playing and singing the blues with sincerity and knowledge of the form. From England, where they had been exposed to live blues when Muddy and Big Bill Broonzy toured in the late fifties, came Eric Clapton, Peter Green, Mick Taylor (all part of British blues guru John Mayall's Bluesbreakers at separate times), Jeff Beck, Jimmy Page, Rory Gallagher, and Kim Simmonds. Stateside were Johnny Winter, Duane Allman, Dicky Betts, Bugs Henderson, and Billy Gibbons. The two pioneers of this subgenre were the best and most authentic: Lonnie Mack and Michael Bloomfield.

Lonnie McIntosh was born July 18, 1941, in Harrison, Indiana. A true son of the rural midwest, his first few residences were primitive structures without electricity. Hearing blues and gospel over the air when he was able to have a radio only added to his musical environment as many family members played and sang country and white gospel songs. His mother showed him basic guitar chords when he was five, and before long, he was hanging and jamming with the local buskers, including some older black bluesmen. One of these, Ralph Trotto, whom Mack remembers as a great player, adept at jazz and blues, took the eager young picker on as a partner, and the duo played in Aurora for tips.

By thirteen, Mack had quit school and was performing professionally. He had added the country and jazz styles of Merle Travis and Les Paul to his blues and formed a band with his guitarist cousin and a drummer. Known as Lonnie Mack and the Twilighters, they played rockabilly, rock 'n' roll, country, gospel, and blues around Hamilton, Indiana. It was at this time that Mack met singer/guitarist Troy Seals and asked him to join the group. Their friendship has lasted down to the current day as they have backed each other's projects many times over the years.

In early 1963, the Twilighters were booked by Fraternity Records in Cincinnati to back a female vocal group named the Charmaines. When the engineer informed Mack at the end of the session that twenty minutes were left over for him to try something of his own, musical history was committed to tape. Mack opted to cut a souped-up instrumental version of Chuck Berry's "Memphis" that had become a staple of his stage show. Taking the original I–V vamp and turning it into alternating 12-bar, I–IV–V, lead and rhythm choruses, Mack fashioned a catchy rock statement that just happened to have the most scorching guitar solo imaginable. Packing up his Flying V, Mack hit the road with Chubby Checker.

When the Fraternity execs heard the driving dance beat of "Memphis," they immediately released it as a single to compete with the jangly surf music of the day. On June 22, 1963, it rocked out at #5 on the Billboard charts. Mack was summoned off the road and back to the studio to record an album of hot covers and cool originals. *The Wham of That Memphis Man* was a spectacular guitar feast of down-home blues, gospel, R&B, and chicken pickin' country, all synthesized into a unique vision of American roots music. It pulsed with boogie grooves, deeply emotional soul singing, and beaucoup chops that put all the Chuck Berry wannabees to shame. With a raging vibrato, courtesy of the Bigsby whammy bar on his "V," and lightning-fast hammers and pulls, Mack was five years ahead of the British blues-rockers who came to prominence in the late sixties. A second single, the V-8 powered "Wham" was let loose as a follow-up to "Memphis" and charted out at #24 on September 21, 1963. It looked like the guitar wizard was ready to bust out of the bar-band circuit when the music world was turned on its ear. In February of 1964, the Beatles appeared on the Ed Sullivan Show, and Mack's career withered on the vine.

*Lonnie Mack looking coy before tearing the strings off his original issue Gibson Flying V.*

*(Photo: © Charlie Gillet/Michael Ochs Archives)*

*Michael Bloomfield spending quality time with <u>his</u> P-90 equipped Gibson Gold Top Les Paul.*
*This guitar would be replaced by a 'burst (58-60 Les Paul Sunburst Standard), and a revolution would commence.*

*(Photo: Michael Ochs Archives)*

Studio work continued in Cincinnati with sessions backing Freddie King and James Brown coming his way through King/Federal Records, but five long years of discouragement followed as Mack scuffled in barrooms and honky tonks. Then, in 1968, *Rolling Stone* magazine published a rave review of the Fraternity album. It being the height of the blues revival, Electra Records took notice and searched him out at a Florida dancehall, purchased the masters from Fraternity and reissued the album. In addition, *Glad I'm in the Band,* a decent album of country rock, blues, and remakes of "Memphis" and "Why," was recorded and put out in 1969. The Elektra connection lasted into the seventies, with the results being mediocre sales and a guest spot on the Doors' *Morrison Hotel* on which he played bass and soloed on "Roadhouse Blues." A handful of underappreciated country and rock albums followed, but by 1977, Lonnie Mack had drifted into a bitter semi-retirement.

It took almost ten years and the accolades of Stevie Ray Vaughan to get Mack a contract with Alligator Records. SRV's knuckle-busting runs owed a great deal to Mack's influence, as he was the first to admit. In 1985, *Strike Like Lightning* burst forth with Vaughan as producer and dueling guitar partner. Mack's vocal and guitar prowess was undiminished, and a new generation discovered what the cognoscenti had known for decades. Two more houserocking albums were pressed, and a triumphant appearance at Carnegie Hall garnered overdue attention.

In 1988, Mack changed to SRV's label, Epic Records. The autobiographical *Roadhouses and Dance Halls* continued his unflagging devotion to honest, brawny roots rock and even had Troy Seals singing backup and contributing material. Unfortunately, his career seems to be in yet another lull as he remains unrecorded since, save for a live album in 1990, *Attack of the Killer V.*

In a business that has chewed up more than its share of talent, Lonnie Mack has been woefully neglected. He still possesses a totally distinctive style that draws on the full range of America's classic folk music, developed from firsthand sources in the backwoods of the country and in the clatter and clamor of city saloons.

Michael Bloomfield came from the most unlikely of backgrounds to become the first *acknowledged* electric guitar hero and a genuine bluesman. He was born on July 28, 1943, to Dorothy and Harold in a rich suburb of Chicago. Raised in an upper middle class Jewish family, his father expected him to be an heir to his successful restaurant supply business. Hearing Elvis and the eclectic mix of blues, R&B, rock, and pop music offered on Chicago radio, combined with a rebellious nature, compelled Bloomfield to start playing the guitar when he was thirteen. He practiced incessantly in his bedroom, to his father's great displeasure, unaware that the intoxicating blues that he heard on the radio originated on the Southside of his hometown. The discovery that Muddy Waters, Little Walter, and Howlin' Wolf were living and performing within a short commute inspired him and a friend to make a pilgrimage to the Southside at fourteen. They could not get in the clubs, of course, but instead listened in rapt awe from the sidewalk. Regular jaunts downtown followed, and before long, Bloomfied and his pal, Roy Ruby, were sitting in at the blues clubs, to the bemused tolerance of the musicians and patrons alike. Bloomfield's interest in the history and roots of the music began to grow as he became a permanent fixture at the jams in Chicago in the early sixties. This academic bent would continue throughout his life as he became a respected blues scholar, as well as an awesome guitarist.

Unbeknownst to Bloomfield, another group of white kids was undergoing a similar epiphany about the blues. With the University of Chicago on the Southside as a base, harpists Charlie Musselwhite and Paul Butterfield, guitarist Elvin Bishop, and singer Nick Gravenites were also haunting the blues clubs. It was only a matter of time before they would all meet, and in December 1964, a demo produced by John Hammond, Sr., was cut for Epic Records with a band that included Bloomfield on guitar and vocals and Musselwhite on harp. Despite Hammond's enthusiasm for Bloomfield, the demo did not translate into the record deal that Bloomfield hoped for. A contract with Epic remained as access to the music industry, however.

Meanwhile, with his father's financial backing, he opened a blues club in Old Town where he got to book all his heroes and jam with them onstage. He and Butterfield also began putting competing blues bands together as an underground scene of young blues musicians developed. In 1965, Bloomfield was asked to join Paul Butterfield's outfit, the seminal biracial, crossover electric blues band. In short order, they played the Newport Folk Festival in July, burning the ears off of the snobbish folkies present with a blistering set, as well as their heretical electric backing of folk god Bob Dylan. In addition, *The Paul Butterfield Blues Band* came out on Elektra Records, trumpeting a new era of electric blues. Led by Butterfield's swooping, Little Walter-esque harp and pugnacious vocals, Bloomfield's daring improvisational escapades and Elvin Bishop's supportive second guitar, with the veteran black, blues rhythm section of drummer Sam Lay and bassist Jerome Arnold, the album turned an audience of rock fans and guitarists on to the seductive lure of hot, hard, electric blues. Just as important, Bloomfield's aggressive and virtuosic playing kicked the ass of almost every other contemporary guitarist.

In 1966, Dylan asked Bloomfield to play on his landmark *Highway 61 Revisited* album. Though admonished not to play "any of that B.B. King shit," Bloomfield contributed hip fills and careening solos to "Like a Rolling Stone" and "Tombstone Blues." Dylan wanted him to join the road band, but, in what would become the modus operandi of his career, Bloomfield stuck with the purer, but poorer, Butterfield band. As other musicians tuned into his vibe, however, sessions came his way with everyone from Mitch Ryder to Peter, Paul and Mary.

In 1967, the second Butterfield album followed to even more critical acclaim. Where the first one had featured energized covers of Chicago blues classics along with derivative originals, the next disc broke entirely new ground. "The Work Song" and the original title tune, "East-West," were long improvisations featuring Bloomfield's fusionary, modal solos. In the course of one year, Butterfield's traditional Chicago blues had edged into jazz influenced, progressive blues-rock.

With the band poised for much greater commercial acceptance, Bloomfield quit to form a funky, brassy big band called The Electric Flag. A wildly ambitious project that never quite reached the potential that Bloomfield envisioned, it did give him a chance to stretch his musical wings. Two albums and a movie soundtrack of soul, R&B, and rock were cut in 1967 and 1968, but the pressures of running a band, artistic differences, and the idiocy of the music business caused him to walk away.

Bloomfield's life and career became the proverbial rollercoaster after the "Flag." A fast friendship with Hendrix, when both lived in New York, kept his chops sharp, but recording sessions and ill-fated ventures like *Triumvirate* with John Hammond, Jr. and Dr. John, and *KGB* with Ray Kennedy and Rick Grech, were disasters. One high point was the *Fathers and Sons* album with Muddy Waters, cut for Chess in 1969. A collaboration with Al Kooper netted some excellent guitar work as did several albums with his old sidekick, Nick Gravenites. But a revamped Electric Flag in 1974 produced the disappointing *The Band Kept Playing*. By the mid seventies, Bloomfield was vegetating in Mill Valley, California with a heroin habit. Harassment by young tyros like Carlos Santana and Terry Hagerty to clean up and play had a short-term effect. He did manage to record modest solo projects of acoustic and electric blues, gospel, folk, and ragtime music. In between, he provided soundtracks for porno movies. In 1976, he recorded *If You Love These Blues, Play 'Em As You Please*, in conjunction with *Guitar Player* magazine. A comprehensive player's history of blues guitar, Bloomfield considered it his best work. Of course, it had virtually no commercial value but was treasured by guitarists.

The last years of his life were taken up with battling substance abuse and playing casual acoustic guitar and piano gigs in California. A decades-long problem with insomnia prevented him from extended touring, though he did make it to New York occasionally. On February 15, 1981, he died of a drug overdose in San Francisco.

Michael Bloomfield was a magnificent blues guitarist. He inspired thousands to pick up the instrument and try to emulate that same sweet, singing sustain and lyrically twisted phrasing. He was a superb ambassador for the blues, drawing attention to the original innovators and their culture and producing albums for masters like Otis Rush. Perhaps his biggest contribution was his commitment to kicking down the racial barriers imposed by a bigoted society on a music that touches everyone.

## SELECTED DISCOGRAPHY

### Lonnie Mack

- *The Wham of That Memphis Man*—Edsel Records ED 158
- *Glad I'm in the Band*—Elektra Records EKS 74040
- *Strike Like Lightning*—Alligator Records AL 4739
- *Second Sight*—Alligator Records AL 4750
- *Attack of the Killer V*—Alligator Records ALCD 4786
- *Roadhouses and Dance Halls*—Epic Records FE 4475

### Michael Bloomfield

- *The Paul Butterfield Blues Band*—Elektra Records EKS 7294
- *East-West (Butterfield Band)*—Elektra Records EKS 7315
- *Super Session*—Columbia CS 9701
- *The Live Adventures of Mike Bloomfield and Al Kooper*—Columbia KGP 6
- *Live at Bill Graham's Fillmore West*—Columbia CS 9893
- *Barry Goldberg and Friends*—Record Man CR 5105
- *Bloomfield*—Columbia C2 37578
- *Essential Blues 1964–1969–Roots n' Blues*—(Columbia) CK 57631
- *If You Love These Blues, Play 'Em As You Please*—Kicking Mule KC 166

# THE GUITAR STYLES OF LONNIE MACK & MICHAEL BLOOMFIELD

Lonnie Mack's guitar style is a seamless fusion of electric blues, rock 'n' roll, and country music filtered through a deep gospel sensibility. Though he possesses neck-bending chops, his lead playing is remarkably free of embellishments, save for his whammy-bar vibrato. He works out of the basic blues boxes with the *occasional* addition of the 3rd, 2nd, and 6th notes. One quirk: he uses a capo extensively, facilitating super-fast pulls and hammers, in what would be an open-string position in the first box of the blues scale.

Track 57 is what you would find on one of his classic blues covers, such as "Baby, What You Want Me to Do." This sucker motors along with scads of sixteenth notes and dynamic repetition. On up-tempo numbers like our 12-bar example, Mack takes few rests so you have to be quick and accurate with the pick to keep up. He plays with exuberant spontaneity, but his solos are always well constructed and logical. Note the theme in bars 5–7 that connects the IV chord change back to the I. And, like all great bluesmen, he knows that the V–IV–I–V changes in bars 9–12 must be emphasized with a climactic peak in bar 9 (the rapid series of bends to the V note), tight focus on chord identity (an F7 arpeggio in bar 10, the repeating of the root, 5th, and ♭7th notes from the C scale in bar 11), and a definite resolution to the V chord in bar 12 with a dominant/diminished bass line turnaround.

TRACK 57

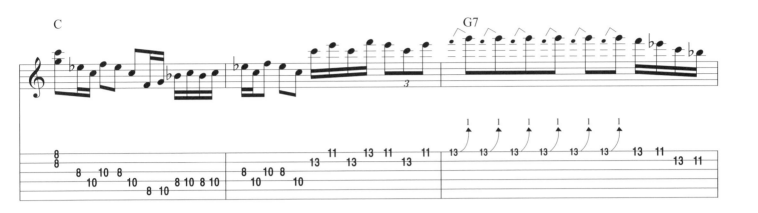

Track 58 shows what Michael Bloomfield could sound like at full throttle. Sixteenth and thirty-second notes fly from this solo like birdshot from a 12-gauge shotgun. Bloomfield could bend and vibrato at any tempo—every bar in this 12-bar slow blues solo has him wriggling and stretching strings like a demon. Though B.B. and Albert King were his main influences, one would have to assume that the high-voltage guitar wringing of Pat Hare was also a factor.

As with all of our previous blues guitarists, Bloomfield felt comfortable in the first and second blues boxes, though he was perfectly capable in the third, or "B.B. King box," as in bars 10 and 11. Also, when playing rock or fusion jazz, he could ramble pretty good up and down the fingerboard with Dorian, Aeolian, Mixolydian, and major scales.

A quick glance by the intrepid student will reveal that most of this solo occurs *above* fret 15. It takes a sure touch to play as fast and clean as Bloomers in these nether regions. Please notice that like Lonnie Mack's solo, this one also contains many powerful, repetitive figures—the triplet benders in bars 3, 4, 6, and 7 are pure hell. By the way, this kind of repetition, along with copious quantities of serial pulls and hammers are indicative of sixties blues-rock.

Though he was a guitarist of uncommon taste and subtlety when he wanted to be, here he is reaching for a catharsis that can only be described as musically violent. If you want to go along for the ride and get the vicarious thrill, start off real slow, being particularly sensitive to the rhythmic values in that plethora of bends. Check out "Long Hard Journey" for a similar fret-curling firestorm.

TRACK 58

**Slow Blues** ♩. = 46

*Kenny Burrell looking for the blue notes on a 1940s style Epiphone Emperor, with after-market pickup.*

*(Photo: Michael Ochs Archives)*

# JAZZIN' THE BLUES—KENNY BURRELL

**S**tarting with Father T-Bone, electric blues guitarists have often had an affinity for jazz. As we have seen, first generation amplified plectrists like the urbane Johnny Moore and the country honking Willie Johnson embraced its extended chordal harmonies and melodic scales. By the fifties, jazz guitarists Mickey Baker and Billy Butler had so absorbed the blues vibe that they were constantly called upon to play R&B and rock, as well as blues. The improvisational nature and intellectual stimulation of jazz, combined with the emotive power of the blues, has always made for mutually beneficial cross-fertilization: uptown looks hip, and downtown looks funky, depending on your perspective.

Butler set a standard for sophisticated blues with his brilliant solo on organist Bill Doggett's "Honky Tonk" in 1956. Baker the bopper played greasy, down-home blues with a jazzman's sensibility with everyone from blues and boogie pianist Sam Price to Louis Jordan. Also in 1956, at the peak of his demand as New York's top session guitarist, he recorded the rock 'n' roll hit "Love Is Strange" with singer Sylvia Vanderpool. Billing themselves as Mickey and Sylvia, their single went Top 20 and introduced many to the thrilling strains of a whining blues guitar.

In the early sixties, the bossa nova and the genius of Wes Montgomery held sway over most jazz guitarists. Wes was no stranger to the blues, of course, but a premature death in 1968 and the financial pressures to produce pop pap prevented him from reaping the rewards of the blues revival. Top-rate jazzers such as George Benson, Barney Kessel, Herb Ellis, and Pat Martino *were* able to cash in their blues credentials in the late sixties as jazz expanded to include soul, funk, R&B, and even rock under its umbrella. The late, great Joe Pass always had a blue streak in his work, especially in his phenomenal *Virtuoso* series of solo guitar albums. Undeniably, however, the foremost bluesy jazz guitarist for the past forty years has been Kenny Burrell.

Kenneth Earl Burrell was born on July 31, 1931, in Detroit, Michigan. Like others in our anthology, he was fortunate to have the nurturing influence of a musical family at his disposal. His older brother Billy tutored him on the guitar at twelve after Kenny had to abandon dreams of playing the saxophone due to its prohibitive cost. His pervasive musical environment extended to Miller High School where the saxophonists Yusef Lateef and Pepper Adams and vibist Milt Jackson had studied. While attending the school, Burrell counted bassist Calvin Jackson and piano man Tommy Flanagan among his friends.

Oscar Moore and Charlie Christian were early guitar influences, with bebop giants Dizzy Gillespie and Charlie Parker chipping in their advanced harmonic ideas as Burrell developed. By 1948, he was gigging professionally in the Detroit area, including a short engagement with both Diz and Bird. In 1952, he studied classical guitar privately, and in 1955, he enrolled at Wayne State University, taking courses in theory and composition. In the same year, he was offered Herb Ellis's spot in the Oscar Peterson Trio in New York. He relinquished the position after six months and returned home, but within a year he had made the jazz capitol of the world his new stomping grounds. Employment with Hampton Hawes, Frank Foster, Thad Jones, John Coltrane, Art Blakey, and Benny Goodman, along with innumerable sessions came his way. In 1957, the beginning of a long and fruitful collaboration with organist Jimmy Smith commenced.

Such has been Burrell's dedication to the six-string lyre that from 1969 to 1971 he was involved with a New York club called the "Guitar," specializing in solo, duo, and trio jazz guitar. Shortly after the club's demise in 1973, Burrell made his new base in Southern California from where he continues doing solo albums, sessions, concerts, clubs, and seminars.

Kenny Burrell is still a major player on the bandstand and in the studio. His brand of smart blues is as timeless and classic as the beautiful Gibson L5s and Super 400s that he has favored. The man whom Duke Ellington referred to as his "favorite guitarist" and who refuses to be exclusively labeled in any one style, had this to say about his roots on his 1968 Verve album, *Blues—The Common Ground*: "The blues is T-Bone Walker, Jimmy Reed, the Staples Singers, John Coltrane, sometimes the Beatles and Rolling Stones or the Buffalo Springfield, and many others. One can detect a blues flavor in a flamenco tune, a Gypsy folk song, in the folk music of most cultures, because the blues reflects the emotions of the common man. It is part of one powerful force with many channels, and that force is the soul of man."

## SELECTED DISCOGRAPHY

- *Blue Moods*—Prestige PR 7308
- *Blues—The Common Ground*—Verve V6 8746
- *Bluesin' Around*—Columbia FC 38507
- *Midnight Blue*—Pausa 9000
- *On View at the Five Spot Cafe* (with Art Blakey)—Blue Note BST 84021
- *All Night Long*—Prestige PR 7289
- *Stormy Monday*—Fantasy F 9558

**With Jimmy Smith:**

- *Home Cookin'*—Blue Note 84050
- *Midnight Special*—Blue Note 84078
- *Back at the Chicken Shack*—Blue Note 84117
- *Jimmy Smith at the Organ*—Blue Note BST 81552
- *Hoochie Coochie Man*—Verve V 8667
- *Got My Mojo Workin'*—Verve V 8614
- *Keep On Comin'*—Elecktra Musician 9 60301 1

## THE GUITAR STYLE OF KENNY BURRELL

Jazz musicians love to expand I–IV–V blues progressions by fleshing out the basic dominant harmonies. Our 12-bar Kenny Burrell blues of Track 59 contains extended, altered, and diatonic chord substitutions for your listening and playing pleasure. The harmonized diatonic scale in the key of A is A–Bm–C#m–D–E7–F#m–G#m7♭5.

Bar 1 sweetens up the I chord by making it a diatonic major (maj6). Bars 2–4 rely on a cycle of fifths, starting with the ultra-sophisticated G#m7#5 chord and concluding on an A dominant (A13) extended chord in bar 4. Note that the C#7♭9 (altered chord) in bar 2 would be C#m and the B13 in bar 3 would be Bm if strict diatonic theory were being adhered to. The dominant chords add "blues spice" to the proceedings and can be substituted at your discretion.

Bar 5 continues with the diatonic major (maj7) while bar 6 modulates to a iv (m9) with the IV chord of D thrown in as added forward motion. Bar 6 substitutes the iii chord for the tonic and sets in motion another cycle 5 (with a diatonic ii) down to the V chord in bar 10. Be hip to the fact that, as opposed to a basic 12-bar blues, a II chord, rather than a V chord, occurs in bar 9, and that a V chord, instead of a IV chord, appears in bar 10. The turnaround in bars 11 and 12 begins once again with the iii (subbing for the I) and a cycle 5 sequence, resolving to the V chord.

By the way, this progression functions marvelously at slow or fast tempos. As you play through it, look and listen for the common tones and voice leading that takes place between chords.

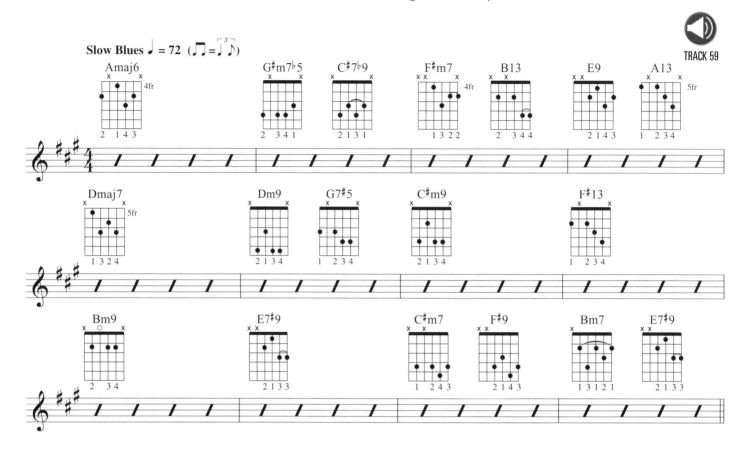

Track 60 is a musical marriage of jazz and blues made in heaven. It is prefigured on a slow blues like "Mule," "See See Rider," or "Soulful Brother." This baby is so delectable that I wish to suss it out measure by measure:

*Bar 1:*    practically "gutbucket blues" (for jazz!), with that "inside" dyad of a third and a snappy, C basic blues scale run.

*Bar 2:*    the IV chord is nailed with a triple stop familiar to Chicago blues guitarists. It implies an F9 chord.

*Bar 3:*    the jazzman's blues scale, the Mixolydian mode, is transversed at a brisk sixteenth-note clip, starting with a cool ♭3 (B♭) note.

*Bar 4:*    more of the same with an emphasis on the 13th (A) to suggest the chordal harmony written above the staff.

*Bar 5:*    an echo of the deadpan F dominant tonality of bar 2.

*Bar 6:*    in case you missed the idea in bar 5, an F9 chord is inserted for punctuation.

*Bar 7:*    a diatonic sequence is begun with a C major (Ionian mode) scale phrased to imply C–Dm7.

*Bar 8:*    the continuation of the pattern from bar 7 with a Cmaj7 arpeggio that modulates to an altered A Mixolydian mode (C and B♭, the ♭3 and ♭9 are added), inferring the A7 indicated above the staff. Hipsville!

*Bar 9:*    a Dm triple-stop and selected notes from the C blues scale suggesting a Dm9 harmony.

*Bar 10:*   C Mixolydian again, but with the notes emphasized to hint at a G minor scale (G–A–B♭–C–E♭).

*Bars 11 and 12:* a "get down" blues turnaround with the C blues scale, an F dominant triple stop and a dyad pattern that would be at home on the Southside of Chi-Town.

It is imperative that you listen to Kenny Burrell and his peers to grasp the refined and technically challenging phrasing of a piece like this. If you are used to picking with *all* downstrokes, you may want to resort to alternate down and up strokes to help you breeze through all those sixteenth-note triplets!

*Jimi Hendrix looking for that Red House over yonder, with his CBS rosewood Strat.*

*(Photo: Michael Ochs Archives)*

# JIMI HENDRIX, BLUES GUITARIST

Jimi Hendrix was so spiritually and physically expressive on the electric guitar that his oneness with the instrument seemed to be a supernatural union, allowing him to reach deep down inside and then soar to stratospheric heights of creative ecstasy. He was, and continues to be, worshipped as *the* rock guitar god. His innovative use of electronics and whammy-bar manipulation are still the benchmark for guitarists twenty-five years after his death. Yet, despite the pyrotechnics and culture-crossing stylistic fusion of his original music, in his soul he was a blues man. He played from the depths of his pain and from the joys of life, from his roots as a black man with Indian blood, and from the heady spirits brewed in the freedom-loving sixties. Had he chosen to stay on the chitlin circuit and play nothing but blues, he no doubt would be considered the equal of Otis and Buddy. Instead he listened to his voodoo muse and created an electric ladyland of butterflies and zebras, and castles made of sand.

James Marshall Hendrix was born in Seattle, Washington, on November 27, 1942, to James Allen "Al" Hendrix and Lucille Jeter Hendrix. As a child, Jimi first heard the jump blues of Louis Jordan, Roy Milton, and Big Joe Turner, with Muddy Waters and B.B. King also making appearances on the Hendrix turntable. By eight, he had become enthralled with the guitar and would mime playing on a broom. In elementary school, he was so intensely focused on having a guitar that school personnel felt it would be destructive to his psyche if he did not have one. He made a cigar box guitar with rubber bands until his father acquired a one-string ukulele. In 1956, Jimi heard Mickey and Sylvia's "Love Is Strange," and his passion to play a real guitar escalated to an obsession. In 1957, he saw Elvis play in Seattle, met Little Richard in his neighborhood, and finally received a $5 acoustic from his father. The hot R&B that he heard would not let him go, however, and he badgered his father to buy him an electric Supro from a local music store. Al Hendrix, in a way to connect with his son, bought a C melody saxophone for himself in order to accompany Jimi. A natural left-hander, Jimi would always turn right-handed instruments upside down and restring them.

In 1959, Jimi was in a group called the Rocking Kings that played the rock and R&B hits of the day. Meanwhile, he was absorbed in the blues of Muddy, B.B., Jimmy Reed, Elmore, and Hooker. In addition, he was impressed by John Henry "Guitar Shorty" Fortescue, a wildly gymnastic local guitarist who had moved to Seattle from Los Angeles. After dropping out of high school in 1960 and scuffling at menial day gigs while living in his guitar, Jimi joined the Army as a parachutist in the 101st Airborne in 1961. He continued playing in the service and met bassist Billy Cox who would later join him in the Band of Gypsys. In 1962, after an "injury" from a jump, he managed a discharge and headed for Nashville to seek his fortune. Two months later, Cox followed suit.

Jimi and Billy formed the King Kasuals in Nashville and slipped into the music scene. They were often called upon to back established artists like Carla Thomas and Nappy Brown and went on tour with Curtis Mayfield and the Marvellettes. Mayfield's unique chord melody approach would later crop up in Jimi's "Little Wing," "The Wind Cries Mary," and "Castles Made of Sand." Other tours included backing Solomon Burke, Jackie Wilson, and Chuck Jackson. While on the road, Jimi met Bobby Womack, Sam Cooke's guitarist, who also imparted the secrets of his lead/rhythm accompaniment guitar style to him. In 1963, his restlessness caused him to move to New York at the urging of a promoter who recognized his emerging talent. Jimi landed in Harlem without a clue.

Fortunately, as he already had a way with the ladies, Jimi met Fayne Pridgeon, an ex-girlfriend of Sam Cooke, who gave him his introduction into the desperately competitive black music world. Jimi would sit in and jam whenever he could, often to the derision of conservative fellow musicians. Besides that, his chronic poverty kept him from permanently owning his own guitar for long, and he frequently had to borrow one to play. In late 1963, to his artistic pleasure but financial dismay, he made his first recordings with saxophonist Lonnie Youngblood in Philadelphia. As he had since picking up the instrument back in Seattle, Jimi practiced incessantly, literally sleeping with his guitar when it was not in hock. First prize on amateur night at the Apollo and the chance to join the Isley Brothers in early 1964 signaled a welcome change in events. At their encouragement, Jimi further developed his funky rhythm chops, snakey blues solos, and showmanship. In late 1964, feeling the constraints of being in another's employ, he quit the Isleys in Nashville while on tour. Before leaving town, he met one of his new blues heroes, Albert King, as well as Steve Cropper, with whom he recorded an unreleased demo.

In 1965, Jimi joined Little Richard's band in Atlanta, but their egos clashed as Jimi jumped back and forth from Richard to Ike and Tina Turner and Arthur Lee (from the band Love, with whom he recorded in L.A.). Jimi was fired, but not before recording "I Don't Know What You Got But It's Got Me." Albert Collins took Jimi's place with Little Richard. In the spring of 1965, Jimi returned to New York where he came under the spell of Bob Dylan's imagery. He became determined to sign with a record company and pursue his own music. To make ends meet, he quickly went back out on the road with Joey Dee and the Starlighters.

Back in town, Jimi ran across R&B singer Curtis Knight who *had* a record contract but needed a hot lead guitarist. Jimi signed a contract that would come back to haunt him in the late sixties, resulting in the Band of Gypsys' album being recorded for Capitol Records in order to release him from his previous obligations.

Mediocre recordings and rough New Jersey gigs with Knight sent Jimi looking for better opportunities. King Curtis, the legendary saxophonist, remembered Jimi from seeing him with Little Richard and offered him the second guitar chair behind Cornell Dupree in his band. As with Richard, the bumping of egos and Curtis's conservative band policies led to the rapid demise of that association.

By 1966, Jimi was discouraged with the uptown scene and decided to stretch his wings in Greenwich Village. The hippies and blues revivalists there were much more receptive to his far-out blues excursions and guitar tricks like playing with his teeth and behind his head. Forming Jimmy James and the Blue Flames (he was not Jimi yet) with Randy Wolfe, later Randy California from Spirit, he became the guitarist that everyone from Michael Bloomfield to the Rolling Stones had to see. John Hammond, Jr., who was working in the Village concurrently, caught Jimi's act and invited him into his blues band. Linda Keith, Keith Richards' girlfriend, brought Chas Chandler to see him. Chandler, bassist for the Animals and budding manager, signed Jimi to a contract, took him to England, and set in motion a musical revolution.

In September 1966, Jimi Hendrix touched down in England, and the rest is truly history. Where the reaction to his outrageous persona and shockingly experimental blues playing had been mixed in the States, the British accepted him as their own discovery. Chandler assembled a trio around him with bassist Noel Redding and drummer Mitch Mitchell. The Jimi Hendrix Experience blew everybody away in Europe and made a triumphal appearance at the Monterey Pop Festival in 1967 in California. His clothes, his stage antics (culminating in the torching of his Stratocaster), and, most of all, his totally uninhibited, blues-based musical assault was unprecedented.

For the next three years, Jimi burned hard and bright with a short string of electrifying original albums and a long, slow slide into the kind of destructive lifestyle that had destroyed blues men like Guitar Slim. The Experience split and reformed, and Jimi played Woodstock as the lightning rod for the counterculture, created progressive funk with the Band of Gypsys, and ended up sucked dry by the conflicting demands of the music industry. On September 18, 1970, he died of a drug overdose in London.

Jimi Hendrix remains in a class by himself. Besides being a phenomenally inventive soloist and master of amplification, he was the ultimate trio guitarist, unparalleled at playing creative rhythm and lead simultaneously. His recorded legacy during his lifetime shows only a handful of straight, 12-bar blues, but underneath the psychedelic haze, blues phrasing and spirit informed practically every note he played. His quicksilver fluidity and feedback-fueled lead lines have inspired yet another generation to pick up on the blues as a way to delve into their imaginations and find salvation. He seemed to know every R&B, gospel, and blues form from the Delta to Chicago to Memphis. Not content to be merely an interpreter, he roiled it around and recast the blues in his own image. Like Robert Johnson had thirty years earlier, Jimi synthesized what went before while pointing the path to a new blues sensibility.

## SELECTED DISCOGRAPHY

- *Blues*—MCA Records MCAD 11060
- *Variations on a Theme—Red House*—Jimi Hendrix Reference Library

The following is a list of blues, besides the various versions of "Red House," that appear on Jimi's rock recordings:

- "Hear My Train A' Comin'" (*Band of Gypsys 2*—Capitol SJ 12416)
- "My Friend" (*The Cry Of Love*—Reprise MS 2034)
- "Killing Floor," "Rock Me Baby" (*Jimi Plays Monterey*—Reprise 25358 1)
- "Hear My Train A' Comin'," "Once I Had a Woman" (*Midnight Lightning*—Reprise MS 2229)
- "Bleeding Hear," "Hear My Train A' Comin'" (*The Hendrix Concerts*—Reprise 22306 1)
- "Killing Floor," "Drivin' South," "Catfish Blues," "Hear My Train A' Comin'," "Hoochie Koochie Man" (*Radio One*—Rykodisc RCD 20078)
- "Killing Floor" (*Live at Winterland*—Rykodisc RCD 20038)

## THE GUITAR STYLE OF JIMI HENDRIX

Though he would lay down greasy, funky country blues with "Hear My Train A' Comin'" and "Catfish Blues," it was on "Red House" that Jimi Hendrix strutted his super cool, bad-dude licks. It was said that you could gauge his demeanor at any given moment by the way he would perform the song, as it most often was the centerpiece of his stage show.

In Track 61, I have attempted to distill into twelve bars a small portion of the guitaristic riches that overflow from the many versions of "Red House." Jimi drew upon the entire history of electric and acoustic blues for his inspiration, with B.B. King, Albert King, and Buddy Guy figuring most prominently in the amplified category.

The regal B.B. always commands his due, and Jimi gives it to him with the rubbery G and B string bends in bars 1, 3, 6, 8, and 9. Meanwhile, the omnipotent Big Albert weighs in with the full-step bend in bar 3 and the sliding sixths in bars 4 and 5. The trills in bar 2 and the double-stop hammer-on lick in bars 2, 5, and 12 are pure Hendrixisms and show how he managed to employ R&B moves à la Curtis Mayfield and Bobby Womack into his blues. The diatonic 6th (E) note implies the 3rd of the IV chord in bar 2. Likewise, those chromatic thirty-second-note triplets in bar 8 give a side-long glance into his jazz roots.

Jimi had total mastery over basic blues and pentatonic scales. In addition, he was quite at home with the Mixolydian mode and other jazz scales like the Dorian and Aeolian. He could dial in at will the styles of Hooker, Hopkins (listen to the acoustic 12-string version of "Hear My Train A' Comin'" on *Blues*), and the Kings, but part of his genius lay in the way he was fearless about pulling licks and phrases from jazz, rock, R&B, flamenco, and classical music and stirring them into his personal blues stew. Another part was his shamanistic ability to extract smoldering, black velvet blues tones from his equipment. Notes on paper cannot convey the sound that seemed to emanate from a place that existed only in his soul.

# PART FOUR: 1972–1982

The biorhythms of the blues dipped into the negative zone as the sixties wheezed into the seventies. Perhaps it was part of the inevitable letdown after such a period of intense cultural and sociological change. Or maybe it was the result of a swing back to more conservative, self-centered times or just the natural waxing and waning of history. At any rate, it certainly began as a fallow season for the blues. Then the emergence of Alligator Records gave exposure to new blue bloods like Son Seals and Fenton Robinson while invigorating the career of Albert Collins. Meanwhile, the *re-emergence* of Johnny Winter, after a substance abuse problem, kept the blues rocking with exuberant energy and unabashed love for the music, even as he reinvigorated Muddy Waters's career with their series of collaborative recordings in the late seventies. By the time Stevie Ray Vaughan shook the rafters with his big, bad Strat in the early eighties, it was evident that a cycle of reciprocal influence had occurred. The blues had impacted on the birth of rock 'n' roll in the fifties and provided sixties rock with its soul. In the seventies, the rock-fueled energy of Winter *and* Collins helped to maintain the blues vibe until Seals injected his dose of uncut adrenaline. In Stevie Ray, the twin forces of blues and rock fused to create the charged environment for the second blues revival that has pushed blues permanently (we hope) into popular culture.

Rock music was having its way with the *sound* of blues, as well. While Johnny Winter started on a full-depth, Gibson ES-125, non-cutaway archtop with one P-90 pickup, by the sixties and seventies he was a confirmed solidbody guitar man. After wailing his way through Strats (briefly) and Mustangs, not to mention the solidbody 12-string shorn to a six-string, he graduated to the loaded sound of a Les Paul and eventually the ringing Gibson Firebirds that would become his trademark. At the same time, his amps went from pre-CBS Fender Bassmans and Supers to the distortion and sustain of stackable Marshalls and Ampegs.

Albert Collins was an early convert to solidbodies, coming into possession of a Fender Esquire, courtesy of Gatemouth Brown, thank you, in 1952 when most blues guitarists were still sporting big, fat hollowbody instruments. By 1965, he was using a '61 Tele with maple fingerboard, jumbo frets, and a Gibson humbucking pickup installed in the neck position. Though clearly playing Tweed amps and then a piggyback, blackface (pre-CBS) Fender Bandmaster in the late fifties and through the sixties, by 1972 he was cutting heads with a loud, 100-watt Fender Quad Reverb.

Son Seals went through a variety of hollow and solid guitars until settling on a Japanese-made Norma (pictured on the cover of *The Son Seals Blues Band*). He had acquired the pawnshop prize for $20 from a hard-up patron one night at the Expressway Lounge in Chicago. When it was stolen, he ended up with the Guild Starfire 6 semi-hollowbody that appears on *Midnight Son* and *Live and Burning*. He also used a blond Bassman for those albums, with the live one, in particular, showing off the rich, overblown harmonics and thick distortion provided by the "ultimate" blues amp.

Fenton Robinson, being the most traditional of this group, has consistently relied on the natural acoustic resonance of his thin-line, hollowbody, cutaway ES-125 with two P-90's, which he purchased in 1959. When the original rosewood fingerboard wore out, he had it replaced with an ebony board from a Gibson Super 400. An exception was on the *Blues in Progress (Nightflight)* album where he caressed a Gibson Byrdland, fitted with humbucking pickups, for a smooth, round jazz tone. Fender Twins have served him well over the years with their warm, clean (at low volume) amplification.

Along with Hendrix, Stevie Ray Vaughan became forever linked with the sound and image of the Fender Stratocaster. He switched back and forth among a small selection of Strats with his "number one" holding sway over the rest. Consisting of a 1959 body with a '61 rosewood board neck, he added jumbo frets and reversed the vibrato assembly so that the arm would be towards the top of the body à la Jimi's upside-down Strats. He also fingered a Gibson Johnny Smith archtop on "Stang's Swang" (from *Couldn't Stand the Weather*) and owned a National Duolian steel-bodied guitar pictured on the *In Step* album. For amplification, he built his signature fat tone around a pair of 1963 Fender Vibroverbs and an Ibanez Tube Screamer distortion pedal.

*Johnny Winter playing contemporary blues on a vintage Gibson Firebird.*

*(Photo: Michael Ochs Archives)*

# JOHNNY WINTER

Johnny Winter exploded out of the late sixties blues revival with a ferocity unmatched until fellow Texan Stevie Ray Vaughan pulled the same stunt in the early eighties. Though he can rock 'n' roll like any ducktailed jiver or heavy metal masher, he is a bluesman who understands the joy and sadness of the blues. Being a white albino in the macho, conservative, cowboy state of Texas in the fifties drove him to find sanctuary in the healing power of blues music. As a lifelong admirer and friend of the late Muddy Waters, he has been the standard bearer for down-home Chicago blues with a swaggering Texas accent.

John Dawson Winter III was born on February 23, 1944, to John and Edwina, in Leland, Mississippi, but grew up in Beaumont, Texas. His father was a singer, saxophone, and banjo player, and big band aficionado. Consequently, by age five, Winter was blowing the clarinet and vocalizing. He also began playing the ukulele at eight, and within two years, he and brother Edgar were performing as a duo, including an appearance on a local TV show. Around this time, his father opined that there were only two people, Ukulele Ike and Arthur Godfrey, who had amounted to anything on that particular instrument. At eleven, he picked up the guitar and began learning note-for-note solos off the records of T-Bone Walker, Howlin' Wolf, Muddy Waters, Chuck Berry, and Carl Perkins. When he heard men like Otis Rush, he marveled at their ability to bend strings with such emotional expressiveness and later committed himself to emulating the technique after hearing Eric Clapton's mastery of vibrato and bending.

In 1959, he formed his first band with Edgar, Johnny and the Jammers, and promptly won an area talent contest. Their prize was a recording session, which produced the single "School Day Blues" b/w "You Know I Love You" for Dart Records. Though a flop commercially, the release resulted in Winter getting called for more record dates with local producers and promoters. A voracious listener, as well as compulsive woodshedder, he made the acquaintance of Clarence Garlow, a local guitarist and DJ. Besides calling Garlow's radio show with requests, he often hung out at the station, spinning blues platters from the archives by the hour. By 1962, he managed to work his way into the blues clubs and got a chance to jam with B.B. King.

A pilgrimage to Chicago in 1963 afforded Winter the opportunity to meet Michael Bloomfield and play at the Fickle Pickle coffeehouse blues jam. Back in Texas in 1964, he cut "Eternally" for Atlantic Records, scoring a regional hit. The notoriety provided him with the opening act slot for rock shows and a string of tours. In 1967, he moved to Houston where he hooked up a trio with bassist Tommy Shannon and drummer Uncle John "Red" Turner. They played regularly at the Vulcan Gas Company (later the Armadillo) in Austin where Winter's reputation as a white hot blues guitarist grew and where he got to meet Muddy for the first time. Responding to the creative rock milieu of the times prodded him to expand into psychedelic effects and experimentation while still honing his blues.

Then *Rolling Stone* magazine featured him in a 1968 article about Texas blues musicians. New York manager Steve Paul was impressed and hustled on down to snare the exciting new blues blood for his famous Scene nightclub. An appearance at the Fillmore East with Michael Bloomfield quickly followed, as did a much-ballyhooed contract with Columbia for a record $168,000 advance. *Johnny Winter* and *Second Winter* were released by Columbia in 1969, as was *The Progressive Blues Experiment* on Imperial Records. The latter was a mixed bag of demos that Winter had shopped previous to his signing with Columbia. It led to some confusion among fans and blunted the impact of his debut. However, *Second Winter,* with its intense energy and drive, established him as a blues guitarist with the velocity of a Texas tornado. Relocating to New York and hanging at the Scene gave him the chance to jam with all the big names, including Jimi Hendrix, who was reported to be in as much awe of Winter as the Texas bluesman was of Jimi.

The seventies saw *Johnny Winter And...* (with ace second guitarist Rick Derringer) blasting high-wattage blues and rock while succumbing to the inevitable substance abuse rampant at the time.

Winter checked into rehab, but in 1973 announced his triumphal return to music with the classic *Still Alive and Well*. For the next few years, Winter was the top rock arena attraction, spewing revved-up, high-volume blues-rock live and in the studio. While admittedly a weak songwriter, he had a terrific ear for choosing great covers, with the Stones being an especially fecund source.

By 1977, he had peaked as a major rock star, and he returned to his blues roots with *Nothin' But the Blues* and *White, Hot and Blue* in 1978. In addition, with the labor of love, he produced and played on Muddy Waters's Grammy Award–winning *Hard Again* (1977), *I'm Ready* (1978), and *Muddy "Mississippi" Waters* (1979). *King Bee* (1981) would be their last collaboration, as Muddy died in 1983, leaving Winter as bereft as if his own father had passed on.

In 1984, Winter signed with Alligator Records, producing three blistering blues albums and kick-starting his career once again. In the nineties, he label-hopped while maintaining a touring and recording schedule with unflagging enthusiasm. Unfortunately, chronic ill health and chronic misman-agement eventually brought him to a point of diminished ability.

Through many ups and downs, Johnny Winter has brought his love of the blues to his fans for thirty-five years. Though it often goes unnoticed, he is one of the best blues singers in a business crawling with guitar honchos croaking out slurred vocal mannerisms. Outside of Stevie Ray Vaughan, no one has played faster or more fluidly, while retaining the gritty spirit and passion of the blues.

## SELECTED DISCOGRAPHY

- *Second Winter*—Columbia KCS 9947
- *Austin Texas*—United Artists UA LA 139 F
- *Nothin' But the Blues*—Blue Sky PZ 34813
- *White, Hot and Blue*—Blue Sky JZ 35475
- *Guitar Slinger*—Alligator AL 4735
- *Serious Business*—Alligator AL 4742
- *Third Degree*—Alligator AL 4748
- *Let Me In*—Pointblank 86244
- *Hey, Where's Your Brother?*—Pointblank V2 86512

## THE GUITAR STYLE OF JOHNNY WINTER

While Johnny Winter is known for over promulgating a surfeit of notes, he is perfectly capable of playing with taste and economy. Track 62 bears a resemblance to his smoldering slow blues like "It's My Own Fault." Winter spends a considerable amount of time in the first blues box, naturally, but here he jumps into box #2 immediately, moving to #4 and #5 post-haste (see below). Again, for a guy blessed with blinding speed, he is an exquisite string bender, as you can see in bars 2, 3, 5, 6, 7, and 10! Be sure to hold them for their full rhythmic value, as it contributes mightily to the flowing quality of this piece. Bar 2 should come under your special scrutiny, as it requires precise intonation for that series of four 1/8-step microbends.

Box 1 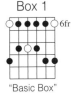 "Basic Box"

Box 2 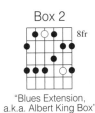 "Blues Extension, a.k.a. Albert King Box"

Box 3 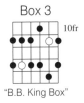 "B.B. King Box"

Box 4

Box 5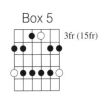

Winter does not lean on the major 3rd (D) over the I (B♭) chord very much, except in bar 8, where he resolves to it with grace. Warning: Those thirty-second note triplets in bar 9 can be dangerous to the health of your digits, and are vintage Winter. At least you get a break in bar 10 with that bend of a minor 3rd, held for two long beats.

TRACK 62

Track 63 displays Winter's acoustic country blues side. Scattered throughout his recordings are a firm handful of open-tuned, National Steel-propelled slide guitar ditties. Like most of them, this 12-bar verse in Open G tuning is in the venerable style of mentor Muddy Waters. As this could easily be considered solo accompaniment to a vocal, the liberal use of triplets swings the rhythm while marking time. Note that the repeating triplets in bars 1 and 3 are phrased like "Dust My Broom," but instead contain the juicy and bluesy 5 (D) to ♭7 (F) interval of a ♭3rd, rather than the major triad. This kind of blues tension tickles your inner ear, briefly and teasingly resolving to the tonic (G) in bar 2 before slithering to the 3rd (B) and 5th (D) dyad in bar 4.

All the tips and rules about slide playing covered in the Muddy and Elmore sections apply here, as well. Winter plays with a plastic thumbpick, but a flatpick, or better yet, bare fingers, will suffice.

*Albert Collins, the "Master of the Telecaster," chillin' and killin' on his modified, maple-neck Fender*

*(Photo: ©1990 Jon Sievert/Michael Ochs Archives)*

# ALBERT COLLINS

They called him the "Master of the Telecaster," and his blues guitar felt like a punch in the ear. His steely tone, pugnacious phrasing, and bad dude demeanor elicited other nicknames like "The Razor Blade" and the "Iceman." In fact, it was the titles of his first instrumentals, "Freeze," "Frosty," and "Defrost" that created the "cool sound" of Albert Collins. Despite his intimidating stage presence, he was a warm and gentle soul who was loved by everyone. It was his music that was sharp, mean, funky, and cut to the bone like a hot knife.

Albert Collins was born on October 3, 1932, in Leona, Texas. His family moved several times after leaving their original log cabin, finally settling in Houston in 1941. Though his uncle Campbell Collins was around playing guitar, Albert was drawn to the piano and organ music that he heard in church. Hearing his cousin Lightnin' Hopkins at family associations and John Lee Hooker on record tweaked his interest in the strings, but he started off taking piano lessons and bought an organ at age twelve. When the organ was stolen, he bought an Alamo and then an Epiphone acoustic, as they were cheaper and easier to come by. The organ vibe would stay with him his entire career, infusing his rhythm and lead with a jazzy swing, even as he fell under the all-consuming influence of T-Bone Walker, as well as Lowell Fulson, Gatemouth Brown, Guitar Slim, and B.B. and Freddie King. At fourteen he began informal lessons with his cousin Willow Young, whose use of open tunings would have a profound effect on his style.

In the late forties, Collins had become friends with Third Ward blues musicians Joe Hughes, Johnny Copeland, Teddy Reynolds (pianist with Bobby Bland and Duke/Peacock Records), and James "Widemouth" Brown, brother of Clarence "Gatemouth" Brown. It was Brown in particular who spent considerable time with Collins, tutoring the eager young man almost daily. By 1948, he was proficient enough to be gigging in the clubs with his own trio. A two-year engagement in Galveston materialized, allowing him to add horns to his group and pursue a big blues band sound that had fascinated him since he had heard Jimmy Lunceford and Tommy Dorsey. In the early fifties, he went on the road behind singer Pine Brown and broadened his musical horizons through the countless blues, R&B, jazz, and rockabilly bands he encountered. In 1952, he acquired a Fender Esquire like Gatemouth's, and a signature sound was born. Shortly after that, Collins would get an opportunity to test it out when he backed up Peppermint Harris (Harrison Nelson) on the Combo label.

In 1958, Mel Young, partners with alto saxist and teacher Henry Hayes in Kangaroo Records, heard Collins at Shady's Playhouse and asked him to back a female vocal group called the Dolls. With time left over at the end of the session, Hayes inquired as to whether Collins would like to record his instrumental "Freeze" that Hayes remembered hearing. Collins had previously shopped the tune to arch villain Don Robey, who responded that Collins sounded too much like T-Bone. When Robey realized that Kangaroo had "Freeze" ready to ship, he quickly enlisted Fenton Robinson from Chicago to cut "Double Freeze." Hayes got the Collins version out first and the big, fat, horn-like guitar blues sold over 100,000 copies regionally. Unfortunately, national distribution could not be arranged, and it took until 1962 for Collins to get the chance to record the follow-up, "Frosty." During these sessions in Beaumont, Texas, Collins befriended the young Janis Joplin and Johnny Winter.

Though he became known for his swinging shuffles and proto-funk, his bands at this time also played jazz and pop standards in order to stay commercially viable. (Collins would just allow his horn men, who could read music, to take over while he comped behind them. This lack of reading skills once cost him the guitar chair with James Brown, as the "Godfather of Soul" was a stickler for such details.) In addition, his blues reflected the groovy jazz found in the organ groups of Jimmy Smith, Jimmy McGriff, and Brother Jack McDuff.

Between 1962 and 1963, a dozen rocking instrumentals, slow vocal blues, and funk tunes were cut in Houston on the TFC, Great Scott, Smash, Hall, and Brylen labels. While he led his own bands for the majority of his career, Collins would, on occasion, back other artists. One such short stint took place in 1965 when he took over for the departing Jimi Hendrix in Little Richard's band. Ironically, Collins was slated to open for the Band of Gypsys just before Hendrix died. In 1966, Collins moved to Kansas City where he played with organist Lawrence Wright and met Jimmy McGriff as he passed through on tour. Twenty years later, McGriff would guest on *Cold Snap* with Collins for Alligator records.

By 1968 he was back in Houston, shuffling and scuffling as he had been for the past ten years, blowing audiences away with his demonic energy and showmanship. Like Guitar Slim before him, he had a 150-foot guitar cable, which allowed him to saunter offstage and even outdoors, to the delighted squeals of the crowd. The blues revival was in full bloom, and boogie redux-ers Canned Heat looked him up while in Houston. Lead singer Bob "Bear" Hite and guitarist Henry Vestine talked to Collins about coming to L.A. and signing with their label, Liberty Records. The deed was done, and from 1969 to 1970, he cranked out three bluesy, funky LPs and crossed over, playing rock venues up and down the West Coast. In 1971, Imperial/Liberty Records went under, and Collins joined the small, Denver-based Tumbleweed Records. One excellent album was produced before they, too, folded their tent. Collins had always maintained day jobs while he gigged, but at this point, he became disgusted and actually quit playing temporarily while he mixed paint and did construction work for Neil Diamond. Collins's wife, Gwendolyn, and Diamond encouraged him to stick with it, and from 1972 to 1977, he just ground it out on the blues circuit between sporadic recordings. In 1977, however, Dick Shurman caught his galvanizing stage act in Holland and, upon returning to the States, hawked Alligator Records president Bruce Iglauer to sign him. Iglauer was thrilled to have an artist of Collins's stature, and the next ten years saw a remarkable aesthetic and commercial run as he recorded (outside of his early singles) the best music of his career. A Grammy, Handy Awards, a movie cameo, TV commercials, and a triumphant appearance at Live Aid in 1986 gave him the exposure and financial security that he had sought and deserved for almost thirty years. In 1987, soon after the San Francisco Blues Festival, he changed labels to Point Blank, where he made two fine discs.

On November 24, 1993, Albert Collins died of lung cancer at the age of 61. He was one of the few great bluesmen to have an instantly recognizable sound as well as style. He left a legacy of taut, tight, energizing blues and dignity born of perseverance and pride.

## SELECTED DISCOGRAPHY

- (Note: Collins' two Kangaroo sides, "Freeze" and "Collins Shuffle," appear on *Houston Shuffle*—Krazy Kat KK 7425, an anthology of Texas Blues 1955–66)
- *The Cool Sound of Albert Collins*—Crosscut 1011
- *The Complete Imperial Recordings*—EMI Records CDP 7 96740 2
- *There's Gotta Be a Change*—Tumbleweed TWS 103
- *Ice Pickin'*—Alligator AL 4713
- *Frostbite*—Alligator AL 4719
- *Frozen Alive*—Alligator AL 4725
- *Don't Lose Your Cool*—Alligator AL 4730
- *Cold Snap*—Alligator AL 4752
- *Live in Japan*—Alligator AL 4733
- *Iceman*—Point Blank/Charisma 2 91583

**With Others:**

- *Houston Can't Be Heaven* (Peppermint Harris)—Ace CHD 267
- *Showdown* (Collins, Robert Cray, and Johnny Copeland)—Alligator AL 4743
  (Note: The LP won a Grammy)
- *The Best of Ike and Tina Turner*—Blue Thumb Records BTS 49

# THE GUITAR STYLE OF ALBERT COLLINS

Along with Albert King, Albert Collins was one of the few post-B.B. King, electric blues guitarists to operate in an open tuning. In conjunction with a capo, Collins tuned to an Fm triad (F–C–F–A♭–C –F, low to high) and played with his bare thumb, index, and middle fingers. Inasmuch as he played most of his lead licks on the top three strings, which correspond to the top three strings in standard tuning, only one half step higher, I decided to notate his music in standard tuning. The only advantage that he gained with his open tuning was the easy availability of open-string octaves (remember, the capo allowed him to play every key as if it was an open-string key like E or A) and quick access to the root on the fourth, as well as the sixth string. "Freeze" is a good example of the octaves being used to give a fat, meaty sound to the repeating tonic notes.

Though very much a "lead guitarist" like B.B. King, Collins was fond of comping behind his other soloists. In case you would like to try his tuning, I am providing diagrams of the idiosyncratic chord voicings that he employed. You will note that his I chord is really a major 6, rather than a dominant 7, 9, or 13. Also, the V chord is a fifth, although you *could* take the voicing for the IV chord and move it up the neck two frets by barring.

Open Em tuning, capo I:
(low to high) E–B–E–G–B–E

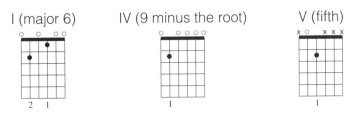

I (major 6)     IV (9 minus the root)     V (fifth)

Track 64 is typical of the cathartic slow blues that Collins perfected during his Alligator tenure. His near mystical command of tension-and-release is evident in the finger popping, thirty-second-note pull-offs in bars 2–4. By the time he lays those piercing bends on you in bar 5 and the combination bend/pull-offs in bar 6, you may feel like you just went ten rounds with a heavyweight champ! Collins used repetition like a mantra, inducing a state of altered consciousness from which only he could bring you back before you nodded out.

He often appropriated the 2nd, 3rd, and 6th notes from the Mixolydian mode, mixing them in with the basic blues scale in the first and second boxes. His finger attack was extremely hard, and he would "sit" on the tonic note extensively. His jazzy sensibility, however, lent an air of lyricism to the combustible nature of his lead lines.

TRACK 64

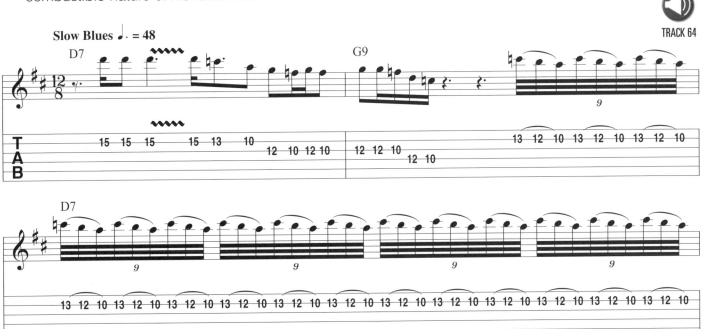

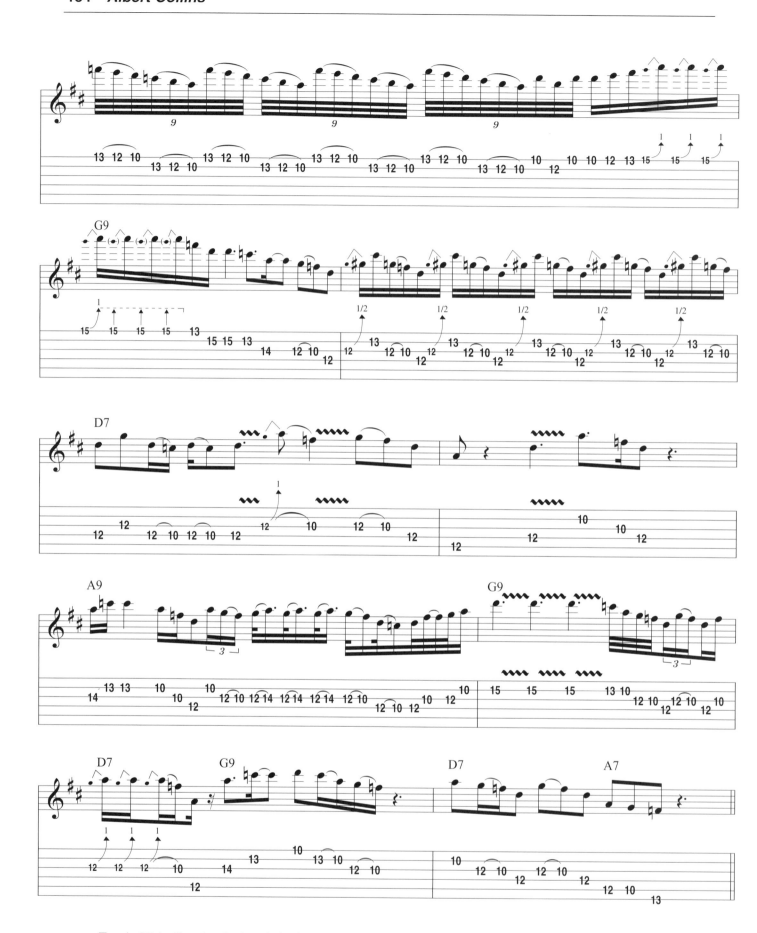

Track 65 is like the I chord, funk vamps that Collins joyfully boogied to now and again. He was not afraid to jam jackhammer riffs into his shuffles and slow blues, but when it came to funk, he left breathing room. Although these licks may appear simple and obvious, they require precise phrasing to get down with the proper, butt-shaking rhythmic feel.

Bars 1–3 introduce the octave pattern beloved by funkateers. Be aware of the accents shifting from the syncopated first and third beats to the bluesier second and fourth backbeats once the improvisation begins in bar 4. The fills *are* simple, but watch when they glide past the bar lines (as in bar 7), giving a seesaw sense of time. If you can think of the octave hook as stone funk and the lead licks as swinging blues, you will soon be moving and grooving.

Albert Collins' sound came from within. Though not a virtuoso and somewhat limited in range by the capo (he often played high up the neck at frets 8 and 10, respectively), he was a blues dynamo. A generous and accommodating man, he could be as ruthless as Freddie and Albert King on stage, dispatching rival guitarists with a punishing snap of his B string.

TRACK 65

*Son Seals crooning the blues to his Guild Starfire.*

*(Photo: Marc Pokempner)*

# SON SEALS

The seventies wobbled in on shaky legs, hungover after the creative high of the sixties. The blues revival had wound down, and Chess Records, once the beacon for Chicago blues, was collapsing under the weight of its corporate acquisition. Wolf was licking his wounds, Muddy was between comebacks, and uninformed critics were ringing the death knell for the blues. Then, without fanfare, Alligator Records, building and expanding upon the quality and integrity of Delmark Records, began issuing fresh blues by unknown and obscure Chicago musicians. The most striking and original of the new generation of electric blues guitarists was Son Seals. Debuting in 1973, he clearly showed B.B.'s inescapable influence, however, the untethered muscularity and naked emotion that burst from his songs was once again the result of the raw, rural tradition hitting the Big Town. As it had in the late forties with Muddy, the influx of primal electric energy rejuvenated the blues community.

Frank "Son" Seals was born on August 13, 1942, in Osceola, Arkansas, to Jim Seals and Eula Mae Dilworth. Jim Seals was a versatile musician who played guitar, drums, trombone, and piano. In addition, he had managed a blues club in West Memphis and opened his own juke joint, the Dipsy Doodle, in Osceola in the early forties. As opposed to most blues musicians coming up in the postwar South, the environment was totally conducive to the nurturing of talent. Through the club, Son was constantly exposed to great live blues and remembers seeing Joe Hill Louis, Sonny Boy Williamson II, and the young Albert King.

Son began his musical education on the piano but quickly gravitated to the drums. He became accomplished enough behind the traps that, at thirteen, he was backing up Louis, King, and Robert Nighthawk. At fifteen, he started in on the guitar, playing along with the records on his father's juke box while also benefiting from the senior Seals's musical knowledge. His first axe was a Harmony acoustic with a pickup, and he often had the opportunity to show Albert King his progress on it, as the future string master rehearsed during the day at the Dipsy Doodle.

Being at home was like attending a blues university for Son, and he advanced rapidly. In 1959, he formed Son Seals & the Upsetters and began gigging around. While playing in Little Rock, he met Earl Hooker at the Chez Paris club. Son would hold this engagement on and off for the next four years, and whenever their schedules would permit, he and Hooker played together. One of the characteristics of Son's career has been virtually nonstop touring, and one of his road trips was with Hooker around this time.

In 1962, Son went to Chicago to visit his sisters and sought out Hooker. The "Earl of Slide Guitar" encouraged Son to stay in the city and try his hand in the clubs. For six months, he played guitar and drums, getting a tantalizing, if somewhat intimidating, taste of the crushingly competitive blues scene.

Returning to Little Rock and the Chez Paris, Son cut a couple of sides for Big Wheel Records. One of these, "No, No, Baby," would eventually be rerecorded and show up on *Midnight Son*. In 1966, Albert King came back through town and asked Son to join his band as a drummer. For the next two years, Son toured with King, recording the epochal *Live Wire/Blues Power* in 1968 at the Fillmore West in San Francisco. This uncredited graduate course in blues guitar ended when Son had to go home and help out after his father had a stroke.

In 1971, Son moved to Chicago after his father died. Jamming with Hound Dog Taylor led to Son taking over his gigs at the Psychedelic Shack and the Expressway Lounge when Taylor signed with Alligator. Son's biting guitar work and tough vocals garnered steady employment, and before long he got his break. In a story that has become a part of Chicago blues lore, superfan Wesley Race heard Son at the Flamingo Club on the Southside one night. Jumping with enthusiasm, he called his friend Bruce Iglauer, head of Alligator Records, and let him hear the band over the phone. Iglauer then went down to the club the next week to see for himself and offered Son a contract. *The Son Seals Blues Band* was released in 1973, containing a varied selection of original, no-frills shuffles, slow blues, and funk grooves. Critical response was warm, and Son hit the road, touring the U.S. and Europe.

After honing his band and new material, Son returned to the studio in 1976 for the earthshaking *Midnight Son.* His first album was an intriguing peek at the fire burning inside Son, but the follow-up was volcanic in its explosive power. Blues and rock critics loved it, and their respective audiences queued up to see Son and buy his record. In 1978, *Live and Burning,* a thrilling live album recorded at the famous Wise Fools Pub, came out. With the decade drawing to a close, Son helped in a major way to revitalize the blues with his double-fisted approach, pointing the way for yet another blues resurgence in the eighties.

The nineties confirmed the worst stereotypes about the blues life for Son. In 1997 he was shot in the jaw by a former spouse and in 1999 had his leg amputated due to diabetes. He signed with Telarc Records and released *Lettin' Go* in 2000 and continued gigging with determination and fire. Sadly, on December 20, 2004, he succumbed to complications from the diabetes and Mr. "Bad Axe" passed on.

# SELECTED DISCOGRAPHY

- *The Son Seals Blues Band*—Alligator Records 4703
- *Midnight Son*—Alligator Records AL 4708
- *Live and Burning*—Alligator Records AL 4712
- *Chicago Fire*—Alligator AL 4720
- *Bad Axe*—Alligator AL 4738

# THE GUITAR STYLE OF SON SEALS

Son Seals gives no ground. He just stands there, feet firmly planted, and plays from his heart. He does not fool you with technical expertise, nor does he try to lull you with jazzy modes. Instead, he just beats on that basic blues scale with unbounded zeal.

Track 66 is a 12-bar solo very much like the exuberant shuffles of "Telephone Angel" and "Four Full Seasons of Love." As you can see, it is almost entirely within the friendly confines of the first box of the C blues scale. No Mixolydian mode for Son, all he needs is five notes! But he works hard to keep it from being boring, and he *does* punctuate the changes. In addition to using the ♭3 (E♭) to set up the I chord, he leans heavily on the ♭7 (B♭) along with the tonic (C). Over the IV chord, he follows tradition and zings in with the ♭3 (E♭) and 4th (F) notes. Over the V chord, he emphasizes the 5th (G); in fact, he leads into the V chord in bar 9 by whacking the 5th on the last beat of bar 8 (I chord). For an urban bluesman, it is nice to see him use a variation of the Robert Johnson, diminished turnaround in bars 11 and 12.

Be advised: phrasing is paramount in Son Seals's music. A cursory glance at the notation will reveal lots of swinging triplets, as well as judiciously placed rests that give this solo wings.

*Fenton Robinson serenading his Chicago neighbors with his modified Gibson ES-125 T.*

*(Photo: Jan Loveland)*

# FENTON ROBINSON

The Japanese call Fenton Robinson "the mellow blues genius," and his jazzy phrasing and melodies are brilliantly conceived. He was Son Seals's stablemate at Alligator Records in the seventies, and the two could not have been more different. Where Seals is all low-down funk and fire, Robinson is refined, relaxed, and introspective. He is a studious guitarist who conveys the triumphs and tribulations of life with smoldering intensity and subtlety. Where others shout and roar, he swings and cajoles with lyrical understatement.

Fenton Robinson was born on September 23, 1935, in Minte City, Mississippi. As with so many others of his generation, he built a cigar-box guitar with baling wire when he was a child of eleven. His early musical education came from juke boxes and The King Biscuit Show on radio. T-Bone Walker and his protégé Pee Wee Crayton were major influences on his guitar style.

In 1951, at the age of sixteen, Robinson bought a Stella acoustic for $13 and hit the road for Memphis where he took lessons from the highly accomplished Charles McGowan. In 1953, he moved to the Tennessee blues haven where he backed Bobby Bland and McGowan in a group called the McGowan Brothers. He also joined the Castle Rockers who played on Beale Street at the New Daisy Theatre and toured Southern juke joints. In addition, the band got the opportunity to broadcast their blues and jazz over radio station WDIA. Meanwhile, Robinson played behind Bland and Roscoe Gordon at local gigs.

When the Castle Rockers split, Robinson moved to Little Rock, Arkansas in 1954 and continued to take lessons when he could. In 1955, he formed "Fenton Robinson and the Castle Rockers" and hopped back on the Southern blues circuit. He got his first chance to record in 1957 for the Meteor label, with Charles McGowan backing him and providing artistic direction. "Tennessee Woman" b/w "Cryin' Out Loud" received little regional airplay but did catch the attention of Don Robey who signed Robinson to Duke Records in 1958. From 1958 to 1959, he cut "Freeze" and "Double Freeze" (see Albert Collins bio for an account of Robey's duplicity concerning these sides), as well as "Crazy Crazy Loving" and the hit "Mississippi Steamboat." Fellow Duke artist Larry Davis and New Orleans piano master James Booker provided backup for Robinson, who then turned around and played on Davis's classic "Texas Flood" and "I Tried." Also coming out of these sessions was Robinson's original version of "As the Years Go Passing By," a magnificent slow blues that would go on to become a standard with Albert King's rendition. Between sessions and tours, Robinson and Davis plied their trade in the Little Rock clubs.

Realizing the pull Chicago was having on blues musicians, Robinson moved to the electric blues hub in 1961. As a guitarist who was rarely without work for any length of time, he quickly picked up gigs and recording sessions as a sideman with the Haveroids, the Five Du-Tones, McKinley Mitchell, and jazz groups like the Prince James Combo. Ever the striving student, he began lessons at Lyon & Healy's music store and with noted Chicago blues teacher and studio musician Reggie Boyd. He jammed and hustled through the years, and in 1966 recorded "Say You're Leaving Me" b/w "From My Heart to You" for the USA label and "I Put My Baby In High Society" and "Rock Your Baby to Sleep" for Giant Records. In 1967, he also cut "Somebody Loan Me a Dime" with B.B. King's band backing him for Giant, where it was leased to and released by the Palos label. The future classic went on to sell over 150,000 copies locally. The worst snowstorm in years hit the Windy City just as the record was about to be shipped and distributed nationally, however, and the impetus to push the single was thwarted. To add injury to insult, pop singer Boz Scaggs recorded the song as "Loan Me a Dime" in 1969, with Duane Allman soloing like mad. Scaggs claimed authorship, had a hit, and established his solo career after having left the Steve Miller Band.

In 1968, Robinson waxed "The Getaway" and "The Sky Is Crying" for Seventy-Seven Records in Nashville. He followed with the album *Monday Morning Blues and Boogie* in 1971. The disc ill-served him, as it featured rock backing and arrangements. Through it all, the Fenton Robinson Blues Band toured the U.S. with regularity. When the contract with Seventy-Seven expired, Alligator Records stepped in immediately. In 1974, *Somebody Loan Me a Dime* was released and enthusiastically received. *I Hear Some Blues Downstairs* made its debut in 1977 with more of the same sophisticated blues and polished funk. In between, Robinson was incarcerated for nine months in 1975 for an involuntary manslaughter conviction resulting from a fatal car accident in 1969. The stretch in stir diminished the euphoria surrounding the critical acclaim that was finally coming his way.

Lack of sufficient commercial success caused Alligator to terminate its relationship with Robinson. Afterwards, he only had two records released, both on the Black Magic label. The lush and luxuriantly produced *Blues In Progress* in 1984 and the equally fine *Special Road* in 1989 stand as eloquent proof of Robinson's stature as an imaginative guitarist and honey-voiced singer. The last decade of his life was spent in undeserved obscurity, and on November 25, 1997 he died of brain cancer in Rockford, Illinois at the age of 62.

## SELECTED DISCOGRAPHY

- *Somebody Loan Me a Dime*—Alligator Records 4705
- *I Hear Some Blues Downstairs*—Alligator Records 4710
- *Blues In Progress* (retitled as *Night Flight)*—Alligator 4736
- *Special Road*—Black Magic CD 9012
- *The Mellow Blues Genius*—P Vine PLP 9001

**With Others:**

- *Angels In Houston*—Rounder Records 2031 (This selection of Duke recordings features "Crazy, Crazy Loving," "As the Years Go Passing By," "Tennessee Woman," and "You've Got to Pass This Way Again.")

## THE GUITAR STYLE OF FENTON ROBINSON

Fenton Robinson's Duke recordings sound as if he had listened to the jazzy fluidity of Wayne Bennett as well as Charles McGowan. The resonance of a hollowbody electric adds warmth even as the overdriven amp imparts an edge of aggression largely absent from his later sides. (Note: Dick Shurman informs that when Robinson once strapped on Lefty Dizz's battered old Strat and cranked it up, he blazed like he was back in Houston.) In its place, however, appeared a greater sense of dynamics and sensuous tonal shading.

Track 67 is a 12-bar minor-key solo whose roots can be found in "You Don't Know What Love Is" and "The Getaway." Robinson has a broader knowledge of the modes than most blues guitarists, but I have chosen to illustrate his command of the basic blues scale in its minor key application, as it is a more accurate representation of his style.

One of the characteristics of his lead playing is a tendency to pick rather than hammer on and pull off. Likewise, he will finger eighth-note triplets or sprightly sixteenth-note runs more than bending, sustaining, and vibratoing. Combined with his structured approach to melody, this gives a controlled yet expressively nuanced patina to his improvisations. For instance, notice how he builds his Am lines (bars 1, 2, 3, and 7) around an Am triad at fret 12. In order to keep from sounding predictable and to add necessary breathing space to the note clusters, he lets the tonic (A) hang suspended in air over bars 3 and 4 of the i chord and bars 5 and 6 of the iv (D) chord. In bars 9 and 10, he accelerates and looses a barrage of eighth and sixteenth notes that pushes the progression along to a satisfying resolution in bars 11 and 12. As opposed to most of the other guitarists we have studied, Robinson works extensively out of blues boxes 2, 3, and 4. He relies on the overworked first box only in the last few bars as a means to resolve the tension of the high-flying previous measures. Though not shown in this example, Robinson often changes keys with the chords as yet another way to express the structure of his progressions. In those cases, he is vigilant to emphasize the target notes or leading tones appropriate to each change—the 3 and ♭7 for major and dominant 7 chords and the ♭3 for minor chords.

It is interesting to know that although Fenton Robinson made Chicago his home for over thirty years, he does not fit the mold of traditional Chicago blues guitarists like Jimmy Rogers and Magic Sam, who show vestiges of country blues in their work. Instead, his guitaring exhibits the technical finesse and swing jazz stylings evident in electric Texas blues.

*Stevie Ray Vaughan mashing the strings on his highly modified, well-used, rosewood neck Strat. Houston, 1983.*

*(Photo: Tracy Hart)*

# STEVIE RAY VAUGHAN

**B**y far the most technically awesome electric blues guitarist ever, Stevie Ray Vaughan was the spark for the new *blues revival* in the early eighties. Continuing the proud Texas tradition of instrumental excellence and innovation started by T-Bone Walker forty years before, he brought the art of riffing and rhythm to yet another generation of fans and players. Legions listened and learned, following him like the Pied Piper of Austin. More than anyone else, he is responsible for giving blues the unprecedented visibility that it retains today.

Stevie Ray Vaughan was born on October 3, 1954, in Oak Cliff, Texas, to Big Jim and Martha Vaughan. Jimmie Vaughan, his older brother by three years, exerted the largest influence on young Stevie Ray through his extensive record collection and his own developing guitar skills. The blues of Jimmy Reed, Freddie, Albert and B.B. King, and Albert Collins, as well as the jazz of Django Reinhardt, Charlie Christian, and Kenny Burrell, was heard in the Vaughan household.

Stevie Ray began fooling around on his brother's guitar in 1963 at the age of eight after having previously considered the drums and saxophone. His first axe was a cheap Gibson hollowbody, with Jimmie's Fender Broadcaster taking its place in 1966. By 1968, he was playing a Les Paul Jr. and had joined Blackbird, a local R&B band. Not long after, he formed the Chantones with his friend, bassist Tommy Shannon. In addition, he began filling in on bass for Jimmie's band, Texas Storm.

In 1969, having succumbed to the overpowering influence of Jimi Hendrix, Stevie Ray bought a '63 Strat and became a member of Cast of Thousands. The band cut one track, which appeared on *A New Hi,* a compilation album of unsigned Dallas groups. Near the end of the year, Jimmie, along with singer Paul Ray and other aspiring blues musicians, moved to Austin, making the Vulcan Gas Company (where Johnny Winter had recorded *The Progressive Blues Experiment* the year earlier) the base for their little community. In 1972, Stevie Ray dropped out of school and joined his brother in Austin. He hooked up with Crackerjack, which featured the former Johnny Winter rhythm section of Tommy Shannon and drummer Uncle John Turner. It was at this time that he saw Albert King live for the first time. King had already been an idol, but seeing him in person cemented his role as the biggest single influence on Stevie Ray's slow blues style.

Austin had become a hotbed of blues activity by 1973 when Stevie Ray joined the Nightcrawlers. His flashing intensity on stage was beginning to draw attention, and a core group of fans assembled for his shows. In 1974, he became the second guitarist to Denny Freeman in Paul Ray and the Cobras. He remained with them for two years, a long time for the restless and ambitious young veteran. The band produced a 45 rpm disc, with Freeman soloing on "Texas Clover" and Stevie Ray wailing on the flip side with "Other Days." The Cobras were big news in Austin, furthering Stevie Ray's following and giving him the chance to develop his vocals. He left in 1977 to start the Triple Threat Revue with vocalist Lou Ann Barton. Barton had just jilted Jimmie's recently formed Fabulous Thunderbirds to sing with Stevie Ray. Despite their clashing egos, Stevie Ray tapped Barton for lead vocalist when he shuffled personnel to create Double Trouble (named for the classic Otis Rush tune) in 1979. In 1980, after Barton threw a drunken tirade at the Lone Star Cafe in their New York debut, Stevie Ray trimmed the band to a power trio with Tommy Shannon and Chris Layton on drums. By now, he had attained Texas guitar hero status. Mick Jagger and Keith Richards had heard him in Dallas, and they booked him for a private party in New York. Though talk of signing Stevie Ray and Double Trouble to Rolling Stones Records was bandied about, nothing came of it. Legendary R&B producer Jerry Wexler, however, caught the band's act in Austin and got them on the bill at the Montreaux Jazz Festival in Switzerland. Though they were the first group without a record to play the festival and were completely unknown, rock icon David Bowie was so impressed that he hired Stevie Ray for his *Let's Dance* album and planned to have Double Trouble open for him in the U.S. on his 1983 world tour. Unfortunately, after completing the recording, Bowie and Stevie Ray parted company over financial and PR-related matters. With their pride intact, the band returned to the Austin club scene.

Jackson Browne, who had also heard, met, and played with Stevie Ray at Montreaux, contacted him back home and offered his studio in order to make a Double Trouble demo. The tape was presented to another legendary jazz, R&B, and rock producer, John Hammond, Sr., who purchased it and brokered a deal at Epic Records. With Hammond executive producing, the remixed tape became *Texas Flood* and was released in 1983. A new era of high-powered, virtuosic blues guitar was ushered in.

Stevie Ray's influence on electric guitarists and fans was immediate and pervasive. Between 1983 and 1990, he recorded a series of ecstatic, guitar-blasted blues albums. With rocking shuffles, Albert King slow blues, Jimi Hendrix rock, introspective ballads, plus terrifyingly fast instrumentals, Stevie Ray changed the face of contemporary music. He also lent his considerable accompaniment talents to albums by Lonnie Mack, Bob Dylan, James Brown, A.C. Reed, and Johnny Copeland. Just as important, from day one he acknowledged the indispensable influences of King, Hendrix, Mack, and Buddy Guy on his playing, bringing deserved attention to the pioneers whom he revered. When he died at age thirty-five in a tragic helicopter crash on August 27, 1990, in Wisconsin, following a jam with Jimmie Vaughan, Buddy Guy, Eric Clapton, and Robert Cray, the music world lost a major star while the blues community lost its greatest ambassador. Ironically, after nearly destroying himself through substance abuse, he had recovered to come back and cut the Grammy Award–winning *In Step* in 1989. With renewed vigor and sense of purpose, he was prepared to continue growing as a musician and an individual. He will be remembered as a shy and humble man who used his gift to ennoble and educate about the music he loved.

# SELECTED DISCOGRAPHY

* *Texas Flood*—Epic Records BFE 38734
* *Couldn't Stand the Weather*—Epic Records 39304
* *Soul to Soul*—Epic Records 40036
* *In Step*—Epic Records 45024
* *Family Style* (with Jimmie Vaughan)—Epic Records Z 46225
* *The Sky Is Crying*—Epic Records 47390
* *In the Beginning*— Epic Records EK 53168

# THE GUITAR STYLE OF STEVIE RAY VAUGHAN

Like his home state of Texas, everything about Stevie Ray Vaughan's guitar playing was big. His large, muscular hands manipulated heavy strings (.013–.056) on a beefy Strat with oversize frets, through fat-sounding tube amps cranked to harmonic-laden levels. His unremitting intensity came from his soul, but his tone came from his attitude of plugging in and playing it loud and straight.

Just like Jimi Hendrix and Freddie King before him, Stevie Ray was a master trio guitarist, skillfully intertwining lead lines, double stops, and chords into a shifting wall of guitar textures anchored to the chord changes. He was particularly adept in the bluesman's key of E. When listening to his music, be hip to the fact that, like Hendrix, he tuned down one half step, making his key of E sound like E♭. For ease of access, I have notated his examples at concert pitch.

Track 68 shows how the strong boogie influence in Stevie Ray's work can be approached. When properly executed, this rhythm pattern should sound like two guitarists, one playing a walking bass line (from the Mixolydian mode) and the other comping double stops for the I and IV chords, the open B string as a pedal tone for the V chord. Be sure to use downstrokes on the bass strings and upstrokes on the treble strings to heighten the illusion of two independent parts being played. This type of pattern has its roots in boogie woogie piano and is most evident in Stevie Ray's "Pride and Joy."

Track 69 is also in E and combines dominant chords and triads, dyads in sixths, and whippy first position E blues scale licks. That ultra cool E9/D chord is the same as the one Freddie King used in the stop-time section of "Hideaway." (Freddie appropriated this chord voicing from Robert Lockwood, Jr., when both string mavens were in Chi-Town.) Likewise, the descending dyads in bar 4 are also nicked from Freddie.

The licks in bars 7–12 indicate a country blues influence, most notably from Texas legend Lightnin' Hopkins. Notice how the I chord is suggested with the root, 3rd, and 5th appearing in bars 7 and 8, the V chord with a B7 broken arpeggio in bar 9, and the IV chord with the $\flat$7 (leading tone) in bar 10. The turnaround in bars 11 and 12 bears a suspicious resemblance to "Poor Lightnin'" as well.

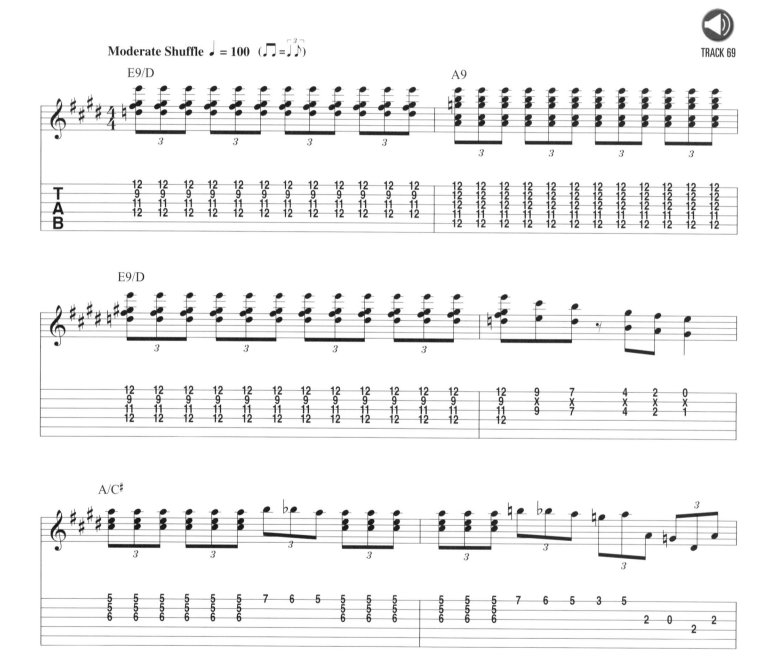

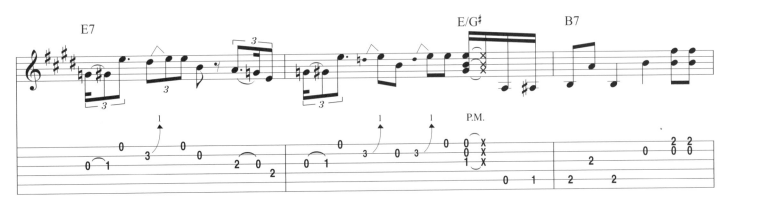

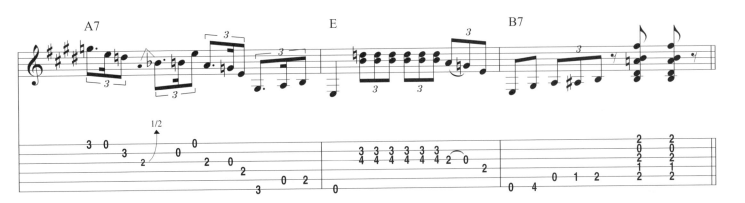

Stevie Ray used the Mixolydian mode as well as other jazz modes like the Ionian (major) and Dorian (minor)—check out "Riviera Paradise." However, one of the main strengths of his style was his brute manhandling of the basic blues scale in each of its box positions. By the discriminating application of major thirds and flat sevenths, he was able to decisively mark the passage of chord changes.

# ABOUT THE AUTHOR

Dave Rubin is a New York City blues guitarist, teacher, author, and journalist. He has played with Son Seals, Honeyboy Edwards, Steady Rollin' Bob Margolin, Billy Boy Arnold, Johnny Copeland, Chuck Berry, James Brown's JBs, the Drifters, Marvelettes, Coasters, and the Campbell Brothers. In addition, he has performed on the "Blues Alley" TV show in Philadelphia and "New York Now" in the city and has made commercials for Mountain Dew and the Oreck company.

Dave has been an author for the Hal Leonard Corporation for almost 20 years and now has nine books in his *Inside the Blues* series to go along with his numerous *Signature Licks*, *Guitar School*, and other assorted titles. He was the musical director for the Star Licks DVD series *Legends of the Blues*, as well as being featured in the *12-Bar Blues* accompanying video for his book that was nominated for a Paul Revere Award in 1999.

As a journalist, Dave has written for *Guitar Player, Guitar World, Guitar School, Guitar One, Living Blues, Guitar Shop,* and *Blues Access* magazines. Currently he writes for *Guitar Edge* and *Guitar Player* magazines and was the recipient of the 2005 Keeping the Blues Alive award in journalism from the Blues Foundation in Memphis, Tennessee.

# GUITAR NOTATION LEGEND

Guitar music can be notated three different ways: on a *musical staff*, in *tablature*, and in *rhythm slashes*.

**RHYTHM SLASHES** are written above the staff. Strum chords in the rhythm indicated. Use the chord diagrams found at the top of the first page of the transcription for the appropriate chord voicings. Round noteheads indicate single notes.

**THE MUSICAL STAFF** shows pitches and rhythms and is divided by bar lines into measures. Pitches are named after the first seven letters of the alphabet.

**TABLATURE** graphically represents the guitar fingerboard. Each horizontal line represents a a string, and each number represents a fret.

4th string, 2nd fret     1st & 2nd strings open, played together     open D chord

## DEFINITIONS FOR SPECIAL GUITAR NOTATION

**HALF-STEP BEND:** Strike the note and bend up 1/2 step.

**WHOLE-STEP BEND:** Strike the note and bend up one step.

**GRACE NOTE BEND:** Strike the note and immediately bend up as indicated.

**SLIGHT (MICROTONE) BEND:** Strike the note and bend up 1/4 step.

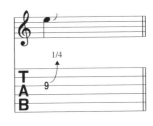

**BEND AND RELEASE:** Strike the note and bend up as indicated, then release back to the original note. Only the first note is struck.

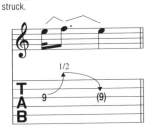

**PRE-BEND:** Bend the note as indicated, then strike it.

**PRE-BEND AND RELEASE:** Bend the note as indicated. Strike it and release the bend back to the original note.

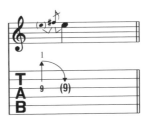

**UNISON BEND:** Strike the two notes simultaneously and bend the lower note up to the pitch of the higher.

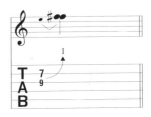

**VIBRATO:** The string is vibrated by rapidly bending and releasing the note with the fretting hand.

**WIDE VIBRATO:** The pitch is varied to a greater degree by vibrating with the fretting hand.

**HAMMER-ON:** Strike the first (lower) note with one finger, then sound the higher note (on the same string) with another finger by fretting it without picking.

**PULL-OFF:** Place both fingers on the notes to be sounded. Strike the first note and without picking, pull the finger off to sound the second (lower) note.

**LEGATO SLIDE:** Strike the first note and then slide the same fret-hand finger up or down to the second note. The second note is not struck.

**SHIFT SLIDE:** Same as legato slide, except the second note is struck.

**TRILL:** Very rapidly alternate between the notes indicated by continuously hammering on and pulling off.

**TAPPING:** Hammer ("tap") the fret indicated with the pick-hand index or middle finger and pull off to the note fretted by the fret hand.

**NATURAL HARMONIC:** Strike the note while the fret-hand lightly touches the string directly over the fret indicated.

**PINCH HARMONIC:** The note is fretted normally and a harmonic is produced by adding the edge of the thumb or the tip of the index finger of the pick hand to the normal pick attack.

**HARP HARMONIC:** The note is fretted normally and a harmonic is produced by gently resting the pick hand's index finger directly above the indicated fret (in parentheses) while the pick hand's thumb or pick assists by plucking the appropriate string.

**PICK SCRAPE:** The edge of the pick is rubbed down (or up) the string, producing a scratchy sound.

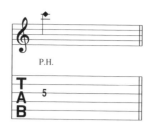

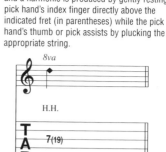

**MUFFLED STRINGS:** A percussive sound is produced by laying the fret hand across the string(s) without depressing, and striking them with the pick hand.

**PALM MUTING:** The note is partially muted by the pick hand lightly touching the string(s) just before the bridge.

**RAKE:** Drag the pick across the strings indicated with a single motion.

**TREMOLO PICKING:** The note is picked as rapidly and continuously as possible.

**ARPEGGIATE:** Play the notes of the chord indicated by quickly rolling them from bottom to top.

**VIBRATO BAR DIVE AND RETURN:** The pitch of the note or chord is dropped a specified number of steps (in rhythm) then returned to the original pitch.

**VIBRATO BAR SCOOP:** Depress the bar just before striking the note, then quickly release the bar.

**VIBRATO BAR DIP:** Strike the note and then immediately drop a specified number of steps, then release back to the original pitch.

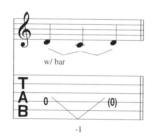

# ADDITONAL MUSICAL DEFINITIONS

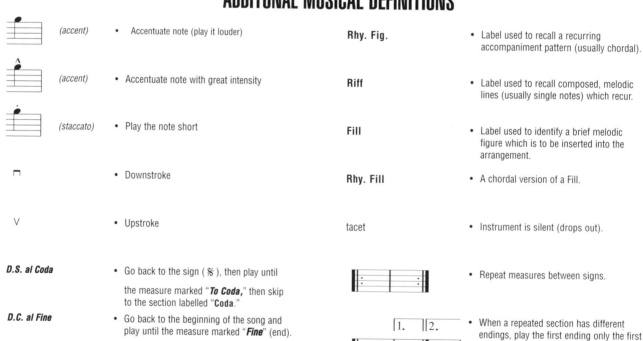

| | | |
|---|---|---|
| (accent) | • Accentuate note (play it louder) | |
| (accent) | • Accentuate note with great intensity | |
| (staccato) | • Play the note short | |
| | • Downstroke | |
| | • Upstroke | |

**D.S. al Coda** • Go back to the sign ( ％ ), then play until the measure marked "*To Coda*," then skip to the section labelled "Coda."

**D.C. al Fine** • Go back to the beginning of the song and play until the measure marked "*Fine*" (end).

**Rhy. Fig.** • Label used to recall a recurring accompaniment pattern (usually chordal).

**Riff** • Label used to recall composed, melodic lines (usually single notes) which recur.

**Fill** • Label used to identify a brief melodic figure which is to be inserted into the arrangement.

**Rhy. Fill** • A chordal version of a Fill.

**tacet** • Instrument is silent (drops out).

• Repeat measures between signs.

• When a repeated section has different endings, play the first ending only the first time and the second ending only the second time.

**NOTE:** Tablature numbers in parentheses mean:
1. The note is being sustained over a system (note in standard notation is tied), or
2. The note is sustained, but a new articulation (such as a hammer-on, pull-off, slide or vibrato begins), or
3. The note is a barely audible "ghost" note (note in standard notation is also in parentheses).

# GUITAR *signature licks*

Signature Licks book/CD packs provide a step-by-step breakdown of "right from the record" riffs, licks, and solos so you can jam along with your favorite bands. They contain performance notes and an overview of each artist's or group's style, with note-for-note transcriptions in notes and tab. The CDs feature full-band demos at both normal and slow speeds.

**BEST OF ACOUSTIC GUITAR**
00695640 ..............................$19.95

**AEROSMITH 1973-1979**
00695106 ..............................$22.95

**AEROSMITH 1979-1998**
00695219 ..............................$22.95

**BEST OF AGGRO-METAL**
00695592 ..............................$19.95

**BEST OF CHET ATKINS**
00695752 ..............................$22.95

**THE BEACH BOYS DEFINITIVE COLLECTION**
00695683 ..............................$22.95

**BEST OF THE BEATLES FOR ACOUSTIC GUITAR**
00695453 ..............................$22.95

**THE BEATLES BASS**
00695283 ..............................$22.95

**THE BEATLES FAVORITES**
00695096 ..............................$24.95

**THE BEATLES HITS**
00695049 ..............................$24.95

**BEST OF GEORGE BENSON**
00695418 ..............................$22.95

**BEST OF BLACK SABBATH**
00695249 ..............................$22.95

**BEST OF BLINK - 182**
00695704 ..............................$22.95

**BEST OF BLUES GUITAR**
00695846 ..............................$19.95

**BLUES GUITAR CLASSICS**
00695177 ..............................$19.95

**BLUES/ROCK GUITAR MASTERS**
00695348 ..............................$19.95

**BEST OF CHARLIE CHRISTIAN**
00695584 ..............................$22.95

**BEST OF ERIC CLAPTON**
00695038 ..............................$24.95

**ERIC CLAPTON – THE BLUESMAN**
00695040 ..............................$22.95

**ERIC CLAPTON – FROM THE ALBUM UNPLUGGED**
00695250 ..............................$24.95

**BEST OF CREAM**
00695251 ..............................$22.95

**DEEP PURPLE – GREATEST HITS**
00695625 ..............................$22.95

**THE BEST OF DEF LEPPARD**
00696516 ..............................$22.95

**THE DOORS**
00695373 ..............................$22.95

**FAMOUS ROCK GUITAR SOLOS**
00695590 ..............................$19.95

**BEST OF FOO FIGHTERS**
00695481 ..............................$22.95

**GREATEST GUITAR SOLOS OF ALL TIME**
00695301 ..............................$19.95

**BEST OF GRANT GREEN**
00695747 ..............................$22.95

**GUITAR INSTRUMENTAL HITS**
00695309 ..............................$19.95

**GUITAR RIFFS OF THE '60S**
00695218 ..............................$19.95

**BEST OF GUNS N' ROSES**
00695183 ..............................$22.95

**HARD ROCK SOLOS**
00695591 ..............................$19.95

**JIMI HENDRIX**
00696560 ..............................$24.95

**HOT COUNTRY GUITAR**
00695580 ..............................$19.95

**BEST OF JAZZ GUITAR**
00695586 ..............................$24.95

**ERIC JOHNSON**
00699317 ..............................$22.95

**ROBERT JOHNSON**
00695264 ..............................$22.95

**THE ESSENTIAL ALBERT KING**
00695713 ..............................$22.95

**B.B. KING – THE DEFINITIVE COLLECTION**
00695635 ..............................$22.95

**THE KINKS**
00695553 ..............................$22.95

**BEST OF KISS**
00699413 ..............................$22.95

**MARK KNOPFLER**
00695178 ..............................$22.95

**BEST OF YNGWIE MALMSTEEN**
00695669 ..............................$22.95

**BEST OF PAT MARTINO**
00695632 ..............................$22.95

**MEGADETH**
00695041 ..............................$22.95

**WES MONTGOMERY**
00695387 ..............................$22.95

**BEST OF NIRVANA**
00695483 ..............................$24.95

**THE OFFSPRING**
00695852 ..............................$24.95

**VERY BEST OF OZZY OSBOURNE**
00695431 ..............................$22.95

**BEST OF JOE PASS**
00695730 ..............................$22.95

**PINK FLOYD – EARLY CLASSICS**
00695566 ..............................$22.95

**THE POLICE**
00695724 ..............................$22.95

**THE GUITARS OF ELVIS**
00696507 ..............................$22.95

**BEST OF QUEEN**
00695097 ..............................$22.95

**BEST OF RAGE AGAINST THE MACHINE**
00695480 ..............................$22.95

**RED HOT CHILI PEPPERS**
00695173 ..............................$22.95

**RED HOT CHILI PEPPERS – GREATEST HITS**
00695828 ..............................$24.95

**BEST OF DJANGO REINHARDT**
00695660 ..............................$22.95

**BEST OF ROCK**
00695884 ..............................$19.95

**BEST OF ROCK 'N' ROLL GUITAR**
00695559 ..............................$19.95

**BEST OF ROCKABILLY GUITAR**
00695785 ..............................$19.95

**THE ROLLING STONES**
00695079 ..............................$22.95

**BEST OF JOE SATRIANI**
00695216 ..............................$22.95

**BEST OF SILVERCHAIR**
00695488 ..............................$22.95

**THE BEST OF SOUL GUITAR**
00695703 ..............................$19.95

**BEST OF SOUTHERN ROCK**
00695703 ..............................$19.95

**ROD STEWART**
00695663 ..............................$22.95

**BEST OF SYSTEM OF A DOWN**
00695788 ..............................$22.95

**STEVE VAI**
00673247 ..............................$22.95

**STEVE VAI – ALIEN LOVE SECRETS: THE NAKED VAMPS**
00695223 ..............................$22.95

**STEVE VAI – FIRE GARDEN: THE NAKED VAMPS**
00695166 ..............................$22.95

**STEVE VAI – THE ULTRA ZONE: NAKED VAMPS**
00695684 ..............................$22.95

**STEVIE RAY VAUGHAN**
00699316 ..............................$24.95

**THE GUITAR STYLE OF STEVIE RAY VAUGHAN**
00695155 ..............................$24.95

**BEST OF THE VENTURES**
00695772 ..............................$19.95

**THE WHO**
00695561 ..............................$22.95

**BEST OF ZZ TOP**
00695738 ..............................$22.95

*Complete descriptions and songlists online!*

FOR MORE INFORMATION, SEE YOUR LOCAL MUSIC DEALER,
OR WRITE TO:

**HAL•LEONARD®**
CORPORATION
7777 W. BLUEMOUND RD. P.O. BOX 13819 MILWAUKEE, WI 53213

**www.halleonard.com**
Prices, contents and availability subject to change without notice.

0606

# GUITAR RECORDED VERSIONS®

*Guitar Recorded Versions® are note-for-note transcriptions of guitar music taken directly off recordings. This series, one of the most popular in print today, features some of the greatest guitar players and groups from blues and rock to country and jazz.*

*Guitar Recorded Versions are transcribed by the best transcribers in the business. Every book contains notes and tablature.*

**AUTHENTIC TRANSCRIPTIONS
WITH NOTES AND TABLATURE**

**RECORDED VERSIONS GUITAR**

**AUTHENTIC TRANSCRIPTIONS WITH NOTES AND TABLATURE**

00694757 Yngwie Malmsteen – Trilogy .......$19.95
00690754 Marilyn Manson – Lest We Forget .......$19.95
00694956 Bob Marley – Legend .......$19.95
00690075 Bob Marley – Natural Mystic .......$19.95
00690548 Very Best of Bob Marley & The Wailers – One Love .......$19.95
00694945 Bob Marley – Songs of Freedom .......$24.95
00690748 Maroon5 – 1.22.03 Acoustic .......$19.95
00690657 Maroon5 – Songs About Jane .......$19.95
00690442 Matchbox 20 – Mad Season .......$19.95
00690616 Matchbox 20 – More Than You Think You Are..$19.95
00690239 Matchbox 20 – Yourself or Someone Like You..$19.95
00690283 Best of Sarah McLachlan .......$19.95
00690382 Sarah McLachlan – Mirrorball .......$19.95
00690354 Sarah McLachlan – Surfacing .......$19.95
00120080 Don McLean Songbook .......$19.95
00694952 Megadeth – Countdown to Extinction .......$19.95
00690244 Megadeth – Cryptic Writings .......$19.95
00694951 Megadeth – Rust in Peace .......$22.95
00694953 Megadeth – Selections from Peace Sells...But Who's Buying? & So Far, So Good...So What! .....$22.95
00690768 Megadeth – The System Has Failed .......$19.95
00690495 Megadeth – The World Needs a Hero .......$19.95
00690011 Megadeth – Youthanasia .......$19.95
00690505 John Mellencamp Guitar Collection .......$19.95
00690562 Pat Metheny – Bright Size Life .......$19.95
00690646 Pat Metheny – One Quiet Night .......$19.95
00690559 Pat Metheny – Question & Answer .......$19.95
00690565 Pat Metheny – Rejoicing .......$19.95
00690558 Pat Metheny Trio – 99>00 .......$19.95
00690561 Pat Metheny Trio – Live .......$22.95
00690040 Steve Miller Band Greatest Hits .......$19.95
00690769 Modest Mouse – Good News for People Who Love Bad News .......$19.95
00694802 Gary Moore – Still Got the Blues .......$19.95
00690103 Alanis Morissette – Jagged Little Pill .......$19.95
00690786 Mudvayne – The End of All Things to Come......$22.95
00690787 Mudvayne – L.D. 50 .......$22.95
00690794 Mudvayne – Lost and Found .......$19.95
00690448 MxPx – The Ever Passing Moment .......$19.95
00690500 Ricky Nelson Guitar Collection .......$17.95
00690722 New Found Glory – Catalyst .......$19.95
00690345 Best of Newsboys .......$17.95
00690611 Nirvana .......$22.95
00694895 Nirvana – Bleach .......$19.95
00690189 Nirvana – From the Muddy Banks of the Wishkah .......$19.95
00694913 Nirvana – In Utero .......$19.95
00694901 Nirvana – Incesticide .......$19.95
00694883 Nirvana – Nevermind .......$19.95
00690026 Nirvana – Unplugged in York .......$19.95
00690739 No Doubt – Rock Steady .......$22.95
00120112 No Doubt – Tragic Kingdom .......$22.95
00690273 Oasis – Be Here Now .......$19.95
00690159 Oasis – Definitely Maybe .......$19.95
00690121 Oasis – (What's the Story) Morning Glory .......$19.95
00690226 Oasis – The Other Side of Oasis .......$19.95
00690358 The Offspring – Americana .......$19.95
00690485 The Offspring – Conspiracy of One .......$19.95
00690807 The Offspring – Greatest Hits .......$19.95
00690204 The Offspring – Ixnay on the Hombre .......$17.95
00690203 The Offspring – Smash .......$18.95
00690663 The Offspring – Splinter .......$19.95
00694847 Best of Ozzy Osbourne .......$22.95
00694830 Ozzy Osbourne – No More Tears .......$19.95
00690399 Ozzy Osbourne – The Ozzman Cometh .......$19.95
00690129 Ozzy Osbourne – Ozzmosis .......$22.95
00690594 Best of Les Paul .......$19.95
00690546 P.O.D. – Satellite .......$19.95
00694855 Pearl Jam – Ten .......$19.95
00690439 A Perfect Circle – Mer De Noms .......$19.95
00690661 A Perfect Circle – Thirteenth Step .......$19.95
00690499 Tom Petty – Definitive Guitar Collection .......$19.95
00690176 Phish – Billy Breathes .......$22.95
00690424 Phish – Farmhouse .......$19.95
00690240 Phish – Hoist .......$19.95
00690331 Phish – Story of the Ghost .......$19.95
00690642 Pillar – Fireproof .......$19.95
00690731 Pillar – Where Do We Go from Here .......$19.95
00690428 Pink Floyd – Dark Side of the Moon .......$19.95
00693864 Best of The Police .......$19.95
00690299 Best of Elvis: The King of Rock 'n' Roll .......$19.95
00692535 Elvis Presley .......$18.95
00690003 Classic Queen .......$24.95
00694975 Queen – Greatest Hits .......$24.95
00690670 Very Best of Queensryche .......$19.95
00694910 Rage Against the Machine .......$19.95
00690145 Rage Against the Machine – Evil Empire .......$19.95
00690179 Rancid – And Out Come the Wolves .......$22.95
00690426 Best of Ratt .......$19.95
00690055 Red Hot Chili Peppers – Bloodsugarsexmagik..$19.95
00690584 Red Hot Chili Peppers – By the Way .......$19.95
00690379 Red Hot Chili Peppers – Californication .......$19.95
00690673 Red Hot Chili Peppers – Greatest Hits .......$19.95
00690255 Red Hot Chili Peppers – Mother's Milk .......$19.95
00690090 Red Hot Chili Peppers – One Hot Minute .......$22.95
00690511 Django Reinhardt – The Definitive Collection ....$19.95
00690779 Relient K – MMHMM .......$19.95
00690643 Relient K – Two Lefts Don't Make a Right ... But Three Do .......$19.95
00694899 R.E.M. – Automatic for the People .......$19.95
00690260 Jimmie Rodgers Guitar Collection .......$19.95
00690014 Rolling Stones – Exile on Main Street .......$24.95
00690631 Rolling Stones – Guitar Anthology .......$24.95
00690186 Rolling Stones – Rock & Roll Circus .......$19.95
00690685 David Lee Roth – Eat 'Em and Smile .......$19.95
00690694 David Lee Roth – Guitar Anthology .......$24.95
00690749 Saliva – Survival of the Sickest .......$19.95
00690031 Santana's Greatest Hits .......$19.95
00690796 Very Best of Michael Schenker .......$19.95
00690566 Best of Scorpions .......$19.95
00690604 Bob Seger – Guitar Anthology .......$19.95
00690659 Bob Seger and the Silver Bullet Band – Greatest Hits, Volume 2 .......$17.95
00120105 Kenny Wayne Shepherd – Ledbetter Heights .....$19.95
00690750 Kenny Wayne Shepherd – The Place You're In..$19.95
00120123 Kenny Wayne Shepherd – Trouble Is .......$19.95
00690196 Silverchair – Freak Show .......$19.95
00690130 Silverchair – Frogstomp .......$19.95
00690357 Silverchair – Neon Ballroom .......$19.95
00690419 Slipknot .......$19.95
00690530 Slipknot – Iowa .......$19.95
00690733 Slipknot – Volume 3 (The Subliminal Verses) ..$19.95
00690691 Smashing Pumpkins Anthology .......$19.95
00690330 Social Distortion – Live at the Roxy .......$19.95
00120004 Best of Steely Dan .......$24.95
00694921 Best of Steppenwolf .......$22.95
00690655 Best of Mike Stern .......$19.95
00694801 Best of Rod Stewart .......$22.95
00694957 Rod Stewart – Unplugged...And Seated .......$22.95
00690021 Sting – Fields of Gold .......$19.95
00694955 Sting for Guitar Tab .......$19.95
00690597 Stone Sour .......$19.95
00690689 Story of the Year – Page Avenue .......$19.95
00690520 Styx Guitar Collection .......$19.95
00120081 Sublime .......$19.95
00690519 SUM 41 – All Killer No Filler .......$19.95
00690771 SUM 41 – Chuck .......$19.95
00690612 SUM 41 – Does This Look Infected? .......$19.95
00690767 Switchfoot – The Beautiful Letdown .......$19.95
00690815 Switchfoot – Nothing Is Sound .......$19.95
00690425 System of a Down .......$19.95
00690799 System of a Down – Mezmerize .......$19.95
00690606 System of a Down – Steal This Album .......$19.95
00690531 System of a Down – Toxicity .......$19.95
00694824 Best of James Taylor .......$16.95
00694887 Best of Thin Lizzy .......$19.95
00690238 Third Eye Blind .......$19.95
00690671 Three Days Grace .......$19.95
00690738 3 Doors Down – Away from the Sun .......$22.95
00690737 3 Doors Down – The Better Life .......$22.95
00690776 3 Doors Down – Seventeen Days .......$19.95
00690267 311 .......$19.95
00690580 311 – From Chaos .......$19.95
00690269 311 – Grass Roots .......$19.95
00690268 311 – Music .......$19.95
00690665 Thursday – War All the Time .......$19.95
00690030 Toad the Wet Sprocket .......$19.95
00690654 Best of Train .......$19.95
00690233 Merle Travis Collection .......$19.95
00690683 Robin Trower – Bridge of Sighs .......$19.95
00690740 Shania Twain – Guitar Collection .......$19.95
00699191 U2 – Best of: 1980-1990 .......$19.95
00690732 U2 – Best of: 1990-2000 .......$19.95
00690775 U2 – How to Dismantle an Atomic Bomb .......$22.95
00694411 U2 – The Joshua Tree .......$19.95
00690039 Steve Vai – Alien Love Secrets .......$24.95
00690172 Steve Vai – Fire Garden .......$24.95
00690343 Steve Vai – Flex-able Leftovers .......$19.95
00660137 Steve Vai – Passion & Warfare .......$24.95
00690605 Steve Vai – Selections from the Elusive Light and Sound, Volume 1 .......$24.95
00694904 Steve Vai – Sex and Religion .......$24.95
00690392 Steve Vai – The Ultra Zone .......$22.95
00690023 Jimmie Vaughan – Strange Pleasures .......$19.95
00690455 Stevie Ray Vaughan – Blues at Sunrise .......$19.95
00690024 Stevie Ray Vaughan – Couldn't Stand the Weather..$19.95
00690370 Stevie Ray Vaughan and Double Trouble – The Real Deal: Greatest Hits Volume 2 .......$22.95
00690116 Stevie Ray Vaughan – Guitar Collection .......$24.95
00660136 Stevie Ray Vaughan – In Step .......$19.95
00694879 Stevie Ray Vaughan – In the Beginning .......$19.95
00660058 Stevie Ray Vaughan – Lightnin' Blues '83-'87.....$24.95
00690036 Stevie Ray Vaughan – Live Alive .......$24.95
00690417 Stevie Ray Vaughan – Live at Carnegie Hall .......$19.95
00690550 Stevie Ray Vaughan and Double Trouble – Live at Montreux 1982 & 1985 .......$24.95
00694835 Stevie Ray Vaughan – The Sky Is Crying .......$22.95
00690025 Stevie Ray Vaughan – Soul to Soul .......$19.95
00690015 Stevie Ray Vaughan – Texas Flood .......$19.95
00694776 Vaughan Brothers – Family Style .......$19.95
00690772 Velvet Revolver – Contraband .......$19.95
00690132 The T-Bone Walker Collection .......$19.95
00694789 Muddy Waters – Deep Blues .......$24.95
00690071 Weezer (The Blue Album) .......$19.95
00690516 Weezer (The Green Album) .......$19.95
00690800 Weezer – Make Believe .......$19.95
00690286 Weezer – Pinkerton .......$19.95
00690447 Best of The Who .......$24.95
00694970 The Who – Definitive Guitar Collection: A-E .......$24.95
00694971 The Who – Definitive Guitar Collection: F-Li .......$24.95
00694972 The Who – Definitive Guitar Collection: Lo-R....$24.95
00694973 The Who – Definitive Guitar Collection: S-Y......$24.95
00690640 David Wilcox – Anthology 2000-2003 .......$19.95
00690325 David Wilcox – Collection .......$17.95
00690672 Best of Dar Williams .......$19.95
00690320 Dar Williams Songbook .......$17.95
00690319 Stevie Wonder – Some of the Best .......$17.95
00690596 Best of the Yardbirds .......$19.95
00690710 Yellowcard – Ocean Avenue .......$19.95
00690507 Frank Zappa – Apostrophe .......$19.95
00690443 Frank Zappa – Hot Rats .......$19.95
00690589 ZZ Top – Guitar Anthology .......$22.95


FOR MORE INFORMATION, SEE YOUR LOCAL MUSIC DEALER, OR WRITE TO:

HAL•LEONARD® CORPORATION

7777 W. BLUEMOUND RD. P.O. BOX 13819 MILWAUKEE, WI 53213

Complete songlists and more at **www.halleonard.com**

Prices, contents, and availability subject to change without notice.

0106